You Can Win Your Ex Back

With The Right Plan You Can Repair What Broke Down So Well That Your Ex Will Come Running Back To You

Written by
Leanne M. Shine

DISCLAIMER

This book is intended solely for dispensing of information
of an educational value for the purpose of helping those
who read it to restore a failed personal relationship.
Application of the information within is recommended in
line with a rational and responsible approach to your
individual circumstance.

If you use the information within to assist with repairing
your damaged relationship, the author and publisher
assume no responsibility for the results of your actions.

Table Of Contents

INTRODUCTION 7

CHAPTER 1: WHAT WENT WRONG? 9

Getting your head straight 9
The truth is in your list 13
What should you have done? 14
An end to punishment 16
Your situation is not irreversible 18

CHAPTER 2: YOUR IRONIC FIRST STEPS 21

Acceptance of the worst 21
Dealing with the pain 23
Do you really want your ex back? 27
The 'Onion Peel' method 30

Accepting blame from your ex can work in your favor 33

CHAPTER 3: THE PATH TO GETTING YOUR EX BACK 37

No quick fixes 37
A planned strategy of repair 38
The New You 40
A mental transformation 43

A physical transformation 46

The comparison date 48

CHAPTER 4: THE RIGHT KIND OF PERSPECTIVE 55

The art of listening 57

CHAPTER 5: THE BIG 'THREE' NO-NO'S 61

Don't reek of desperation 61
The key to not appearing desperate is calm intention 61

The 'urgent, 'important, and 'guilt' mistakes 63

Desperation mistake #1: Pleading and begging 64

Desperation mistake #2: Claiming it's important 64

Desperation mistake #3: Putting on the guilt. 64

Don't cling to your ex 65

The key to not appear as if you're still clinging 65

Stop trying to control the situation 66
The key to showing you're in control 66

CHAPTER 6: CONTACT STRATEGIES **69**

The ideal time to contact 69
The ideal method of contact 71
What to say in your initial contact 73
Don't set up a meeting time 75

You don't want a reply 75

You don't want your ex back 76

Write in a friendly, pleasant tone 76

Keep your letter short 77

Keep it 90% focused on you, 10% on your ex 77

Taking complete responsibility 78

It's time to move on 79

Something 'good' has happened 79

The 'my time with you was the best' approach 81
How to get your ex to return your messages 85
When you don't get a response 89

CHAPTER 7: RESPONSE STRATEGIES **93**

When to return their contact 93
I see how you feel 94
What to do if your ex has met someone else 95

When to suggest a get together? 100
Hooking up again and what to avoid 102
Three's a crowd and familiarity is old 102

Raising issues 103

"We were great, but not that great" 105
The all knowing thirty party 108

CHAPTER 8: PSYCHOLOGICAL WEAPONS **111**

The Power of Saying "I Won't Let Myself Miss You" 111
Misery is the deal breaker; happiness the deal maker. 113
The longer the distance, the greater the pull 116
The projection method 118
Something has changed... 120
CHAPTER 9: THE SECOND CHANCE **123**

"I'm not ready yet"... 123
Deciding there will be a second chance 125
A first date, again 128
You're back together 130

Introduction

Losing your partner is one of the hardest things you'll ever have to endure. The moment they disappear through the door it literally feels like the world begins to crash down all around you. It can be both mentally and physically crippling and leave you contemplating all kinds of thoughts that you never thought you'd have - that you never wanted to have. Or, just as commonly, you can lose the ability to think clearly at all as you become lost in a haze of despair and uncertainty.

To those who have never experienced abandonment at the hands of a loved one it is hard to fully grasp the degree to which it hurts and the extent to which the pain it sends your way can debilitate and consume every moment of your life.

"There's plenty of fish in the ocean," they'll say.
"You'll get over it, don't worry about it, just move on," others will add.
"They didn't deserve you anyway, their loss."

Such advice may be well-meaning and even accurate but it's usually not very helpful if all you want is for the person you love to come back into your life. Yes, there are plenty of people out there that might replace your partner, but right about now there's only one person you can think of. Maybe it really is "their loss", but if that were true why does your heart feel like it is being squashed in a vice? Yes, you'll get over it one way or the other, but you can't just move on while there's a chance that, if you play your cards right, you can mend things and restore your relationship.

The truth is any relationship that is truly special is worth trying to salvage. Anyone who tells you otherwise is wrong. It doesn't matter if you've already broken up and things seem like a lost cause. When it hurts as bad as I'm guessing it's hurting you right now, know that the pain you're feeling is your heart telling you that *what you had was special and you don't want to lose it.* But guess what: if you give up now or make all the wrong choices while trying to save it, you will lose your ex forever.

This book has been written to help make sure that doesn't happen to you.

Chapter 1: What went wrong?

Getting your head straight

The moment you lose something as precious as your life-partner it is only natural to want to take immediate action to try to persuade him or her to return. But despite what you think, you're not ready to do that yet.

Before you take any action at all that *involves your ex* you must first get your head on straight. Many people have lost the love of their life by making rash decisions and taking spur of the moment actions without first taking a little time to get their mind straight. It's sad because in many of these cases they could have saved their relationships by just taking a little time to pause and think.

Don't be one of them. Don't live the rest of your life with regret because you allowed a moment of desperation to dictate your next move. Don't destroy your chances of getting back together by letting the fear of never getting your ex back influence you to do or say the wrong thing at the wrong time. And let's be clear, right now *is the wrong time* to do or say virtually anything at all to your ex. At this very moment in time your internal and external dialogue needs to be directed not at your ex but at yourself.

Think of your lost relationship as being similar to an open fire. When the fire is burning bright it is much easier to keep going as there is plenty of flame to catch on to new wood, but as the fire begins to dwindle it becomes harder to keep alight. When the fire almost dies, there may be a few embers left that can be used to reignite the fire, but you must use them carefully. Rather than simply throw a large chunk of wood on those embers, you need to add tinder, fan them, and allow a small flame to catch, allow it to grow, and slowly nurture it into a larger flame before it will once again catch the chunk of wood and burn bright again. A failure to grow the embers slowly but steadily will see them die at which point any chance of creating another full and brightly burning fire will be lost.

If you try to save your relationship but fail to take the time to get your head straight, it will be just like throwing a large chunk of wood on dwindling embers. The chance it will catch will be virtually zero but the chance the fire will die completely will be high indeed, if not a given.

Before we continue, it is important that you don't confuse "getting your head straight" with "getting over your ex." At this moment in time you're hurting and no amount of thinking, planning, understanding or awareness is going to change that, at least, not overnight. So don't expect it to. Don't place pressure on yourself right now to achieve anything. When we say it's time to get your head on straight, we mean it's time to *start the process*, nothing more. So let's start.

Straws on the camel's back

The very first thing you need to do to help get your head on straight is to sit down and brainstorm a list of all the things that you can possibly think of that contributed to your partner leaving you. To do this you'll need a pen and paper, or maybe lots of paper. Don't be tempted to type away on a computer. There is a very real benefit to using a pen and paper; it is a slower and more physically tangible process that registers more deeply in your subconscious as you do it. Typing on a keyboard and looking at a screen just doesn't have the same effect on your mind and nor will it help jog your memory in the same way that all the very fine mechanical movements of handwriting will.

Make sure you are alone, likely to be uninterrupted, and that you are surrounded by silence. Don't have your favorite sad music playing or the TV running. You will want to be completely alone with nothing but your own thoughts and the paper in front of you.

But most of all you need to be honest. What you write is for your eyes only so make it as honest as can be. Remind yourself that you're not trying to blame your ex or blame yourself. Cast your mind back to your relationship as if you were a fly on the wall or as if you were a third party counselor, examining the relationship "as is" devoid of emotion. It will be hard for you are currently filled with all kinds of emotions related to your loss, but it is very important that you exercise nothing but honesty as you write your list. Don't let yourself fall into blaming anyone; just identify every issue you can think of that worked to harm your relationship with your ex.

Now, it is important to realize that there is no such thing as a great relationship ending because of one single thing. For example, did your relationship end because you were caught cheating on your partner? Then know your cheating didn't end the relationship - there were reasons why you allowed yourself to cheat and it is those reasons that ended the relationship - possibly amongst many other reasons too. In this example, the cheating was merely the final straw that broke the camel's back but up until that point there were other straws that were weighing the relationship down.

The writing is always visible on the wall prior to a relationship breakdown. Sometimes it is visible to both partners for a long time prior to the eventual break while other times it is only visible to one partner. But in nearly all cases the writing becomes clearly visible once the relationship ends. For example, it is common for partners who have been cheated on to say, "I knew it, I knew something was wrong for months, but I just couldn't pinpoint it, but now it's all so clear..." before elaborating on all the events that made the fact their partner was having an affair actually quite obvious.

Let's use the issue of one partner having an affair to illustrate the kinds of points - straws - that you may write down as reasons why things went wrong and he or she left you:

- I stopped giving her my attention months ago and was spending way too much time at the bar with my buddies.
- I've been flirting with other women right in front of her; she probably thought I was cheating too
- I let myself get too stressed about money and took it out on her, instead of working with her to get through our problems
- She kept saying she wanted kids and the clock was ticking, and I kept joking "you better look elsewhere, because I don't"
- I used to give her flowers every Wednesday, then I just stopped

There's no need to continue with this example list as by now you should be able to see that *whatever reason you can think of* you should write down. It doesn't matter if it's right or wrong - if it comes to mind, write it down. This exercise is about helping you get your head straight by allowing all the reasons that are in your head about what could possibly have harmed your relationship to come out right now in a controlled and private environment. It is far better to blurt out what isn't accurate, or even what is, privately than it is to blurt it out to your ex without thinking through the ramifications first. By brainstorming this list now, you'll be starting the process of coming to terms with the reality behind what caused your situation, even if your list doesn't exactly clarify it just yet.

If you get stuck, ask yourself questions like: "What did I do that she didn't like?" or "What can I think of that I shouldn't have done?" or "What could I have done better?" or "Is there anything I can remember that she asked of me that I ignored?" Then write down your answers.

The truth is in your list

Remember, the key to creating your list of possible reasons that contributed to ruin your relationship is to ignore blaming anyone in favor of just being honest about the many things that you (or they) did that worked against rather than for a healthy relationship. If you're honest, and if you've written everything down that comes to mind, then your list should be filled with a number of things that you said or did - or didn't say or didn't do - that may have added up as straws to break the camel's back. Remind yourself that it's never one thing that ends a relationship; it is always many things compounded. The "one thing" you think caused your breakup is usually just the final straw.

For this reason, the list you now hold in your hands is extremely important to the future of your relationship with your ex. The items you've brainstormed may each have contributed to your ex leaving you. Sure, some of the items on this list may have little or no bearing on your ex's decision to leave but the mere fact that you included them on the list is an indication that you feel they may have. For this reason they are important because, as you will see later, restoring your relationship is of no value if you are unable to prevent yourself from walking down the same path again and ruining it once and for all.

Review everything on your list. Don't critique any item, or cross any item off just yet. Just review it. As you do, be sure to write down any additional thoughts or items that come to mind. Keep doing this until you feel your list is extensive and covers everything that may have worked to sour what you had with your ex.

What should you have done?

Here's the truth: most relationships end without the truth as to why it ended being discussed openly between both partners. In all likelihood, your ex has walked out on you without having communicated his or her true feelings about why they're walking out. If they did communicate a reason, it was probably easier just to tell you about the "final straw" than it was to tell you all of the reasons that really forced their hand, many of which may now be on the list before you.

Did you know that it is also common for partners to do something bad so that they can get out of a relationship easier than if they had to own up to the many reasons why they wanted to leave in the first place? Many people will cheat on their partners and allow themselves to be caught as the easy way out. It's much easier to do that than to criticize someone's personal qualities directly. Both men and women do this often, sometimes consciously, sometimes unconsciously.

We started the process of writing down these reasons not to lay blame but to help bring clarity to your mind about the causes behind what pushed your ex away. Your ex will probably never tell you the truth if the reason they left relates to your personal qualities and this is especially the case if your relationship was special and loving. As ironic as it is, sometimes it is easier to hurt someone by doing something that you know they won't like than by telling them that they are doing many things that you don't like.

Remind yourself right now that the real reasons your relationship ended are probably on your list. Even if this is incorrect - even if the real reasons are completely unrelated to you or you have failed to pinpoint them - there's no other way you can find out what they are *right at this moment*. All you can do, for now, is to move forward on the basis that it will be helpful to find out what things you could have said and done better in the past so that you can do so in the future. If the things on your list did contribute to harming your relationship, they won't again. If they didn't, then they won't harm any future relationship you establish, whether it is with your ex or someone else entirely.

You can't change the past; whatever in the past sent your ex packing is now completely out of your control. It's done and there's no going back; there's only going forward and the first step to *going forward constructively* is to identify not what happened in the past that you <u>had</u> control over but *what should have happened that you <u>have</u> control over*.

To do this, take a fresh piece of a paper and draw two columns. In the first column, write the first thing from your list into it. In the second column, write down what you think *you should have said or done differently.*

For example, let's look at the first item from our previous example list:

What went wrong	What should have happened
I stopped giving her my attention months ago and was spending way too much time at the bar with my buddies.	I should have given her my complete devotion. If I was at the bar with my friends she should have been with me. If not, it should have been rare. I should have made it clear that she was more important to me than drinks, bars, or even my friends. I should have shown more interest in being with her than being anywhere without her. I should have made her feel special.

Now, repeat this process with *every single item on your list.*

An end to punishment

By now you will have two lists. One that details all the things you think you said or did, or didn't, that harmed your relationship. The second list takes everything from the first and flips it over to its reverse creating a list of all the things you know you should have done better *and will from now on.*

Now, screw up the first list and throw it in the bin. Taking this action sends a clear message to your subconscious mind that the items on that list no longer matter.

You see, the problem with creating a list like the one you just threw away is the tendency you'll have to blame yourself for everything on the list. Throwing away the list is also a step in respecting the truth that blame is completely irrelevant now. You can blame yourself until you're blue in the face but that won't change the fact that your ex has left you. Or, you can blame your ex, and again, nothing will change. All blame gives you is negative feelings, thoughts and emotions that do nothing to help your cause.

Right now, say out loud:

> *"Punishment ends now. I won't punish myself or my ex for what has happened from this point forward. I won't blame myself, or blame my ex for anything that happened in the past. From now on, the only thing that matters is to think and act constructively, now and in the future."*

If necessary, repeat this aloud many times until you can repeat it without reading it.

Was the breakup your fault? It doesn't matter. Was it your ex's fault? It doesn't matter. What matters is this: *that you learn from what has happened so that you can take control of yourself to ensure it doesn't happen again because of anything you do or say.*

Don't skip over this advice lightly for it is the very approach you need to stave off arguments, end future fights, and put yourself in a powerful state of mind to move towards attracting your ex back. Any kind of statement or action that revolves around blame or punishment is destructive to your goal of winning your ex back. From now on you must keep your mind on nothing but the task at hand - winning your ex back - and to succeed you must remain in a constructive frame of mind. The first step to doing that is to get past blame, guilt or the need to punish whoever was responsible.

Your situation is not irreversible

Now that you're clear on what you think went wrong and what you should have done instead, realize that nothing that did go wrong is irreversible. Sure, you can't change the fact that it did go wrong and that whatever happened resulted in your ex walking out the door. But, that also doesn't change the fact that absolutely everything on your remaining list that you feel you should or could have done *you can still do.*

But not right away; not right now.

Instead, you need to take time out. You need to take more time than what it has taken you to compile your list; more time to review your list over and over again and burn into your mind all those things that you should have done; more time to truly leave the blame side of the equation behind in your mind, and more time to get your head straight about what you're going to do and how you're going to act moving forward. This is absolutely crucial because *these are things you are going to have to do in the future* and not just once here and there, but permanently as a way of life.

Now, if you are sitting there thinking this is wrong, that everything isn't irreversible, that it's all too late - that you're on your own - then ask yourself why are you reading a guide on how to get your ex back? If you didn't think there was a chance, even a slim one, why would you have bothered to have picked up this guide? The answer is simple: somewhere inside you think there's a chance or, at the very least, you hope there's a chance. In both cases you can either walk away now or let your ex disappear forever, or you can make an effort to see whether or not that inner hope you have can be turned into the reality you truly want. Ask yourself, if your ex is truly the person you want to share your life with, isn't it worth it to try to win them back?

If you're answer is "no", then you don't really want your ex back. Sure, you're hurting, but in the end you know in your heart that you really didn't want to spend your life with your ex anyway. If that's the case, then I suggest you read the rest of this book to help you learn a few things about how not to let your next relationship go down the same path as your last one.

But I'm guessing your answer is "yes" and so it should be, for all great relationships are worth every effort you can muster to repair, save, and rebuild into the joy of companionship and sharing that they should be.

Unfortunately, the next step to achieving just that is actually the hardest step of all.

Chapter 2: Your Ironic First Steps

Acceptance of the worst

What is the one thing you absolutely don't want right now? The answer is pretty obvious isn't it: you don't want to lose your ex forever! In fact, you don't want to lose them so badly that you're willing to do anything, anything at all, to get them back, right?

The problem is if you truly are willing to do absolutely anything to win back your ex then you are at the risk of doing the very thing that will push them away further. The moment we are willing to do anything we are also able to do anything, and usually that is because the driving motive that makes us so willing is such a strong emotional one. Be willing to do anything, yes, but first think it through. Strong emotions cloud our ability to act rationally, and it is under that cloud that mistakes get made.

To avoid such mistakes you must take a leap of faith that will go against the grain of everything you want in life right now, but it is absolutely essential that you do so.

You must accept, right now, that your ex is not coming back to you. Your ex left you and now, for better or for worse, you are single. Your ex is going their own way, and so are you.

Right now, say out loud:

> *"[Your ex's name] has left and now I'm free to do as I please.*

[Your ex's name] has left me and is not coming back, and I accept that [your ex's name] is also free to live his/her life as he/she chooses. We have gone our separate ways and even though I'll miss him/her, I'm good with that now."

It will be really hard to say those words and you will probably burst into tears as you do it. But you *must* do it. Say it out loud for as many times as is necessary for the words to begin to resonate as the truth.

Why do you have to do this? Isn't this counter-productive to your goal of winning your ex back? No! It is essential to bolster your chances of winning your ex back because a failure to accept that your ex may never return is the primary reason behind why many people unconsciously wreck any chance they ever had of rekindling their relationship! By setting your mind up right from the start our intention is to make sure that it doesn't become your number one reason for ruining your future chance with your ex too!

Until such time as you accept the possibility that no matter what you do your ex may never return, you relinquish control of intelligent rational response and hand it over to your emotions. You may think you're in control, then BAM - out of nowhere fear or desperation will lead you to say or do exactly the wrong thing at the wrong time and end any chance you ever had of restoring your relationship. You're not going to let that happen, are you? Acceptance is the beginning of taking back your power.

The fact is right now, at this very moment, you are single and your ex is gone.

You must accept this, no matter how badly it hurts.

Even though our goal together is to fix your relationship and win your ex back, the only way this can be done intelligently, thoughtfully and correctly is to start from a clean slate and move from there. That "clean slate" is the foundation of your future success and it is a foundation that must begin not from the relationship you once had, but with the new relationship you will have in the future.

You need to sever the tie to that old failed relationship, and let's face it, that's something you seriously WANT to do - after all, it didn't work! Don't cling to what is broken! Accept that the old and now broken relationship that didn't work is gone. Tell yourself right now that if you don't accept your partner is gone and isn't coming back you'll never get the chance to start anew with them. This may be an ironic step towards achieving your goal, but it is a very important one. Don't underestimate its importance.

Dealing with the pain

One of the biggest roadblocks to getting your mind straight is to accept your partner is gone, you're now single and that your partner is never coming back. This roadblock is held in place rather firmly by the pain that you're presently experiencing.

You don't need me to tell you that the pain of being left by your ex is excruciating. I've been there too. It feels like the whole world has been drained of color. Songs you used to like become dull and songs you never noticed before become prominent, especially those with lyrics that sound like they're describing exactly what has happened to you. Everywhere you turn you hear music, from shopping centers to the TV, and every time you do it's virtually impossible not to hear the story of your miserable love life getting replayed. It feels like you can't escape the memories and you can't escape the misery.

It's not just emotional turmoil you're suffering either. When you truly love someone and lose them, your whole body sinks like a lead weight. You lose all your energy with all your emotions and constant thought about the situation at hand, and before long you are barely able to physically function. Worse, drinking alcohol and binging on junk food often follows and before you know it you're not only suffering immense mental and physical pain but you're spiraling out of good health into a world of chronic illness. Again, I've been there.

In serious cases you can even start believing the chatter in your own mind that "you can't live without your ex" and, when it seems like you're going to have to do just that, it is all too easy to start thinking thoughts of suicide. The more depressed you get the more you begin to think about it. Again, I've been there.

And you're probably there or somewhere along that road, right now.

First, know that while it feels like a cold and lonely place, you're not alone. Right now, all over the world, there are thousands of people going through exactly what you're going through, just as there have been in the past and will also be in the future. You feel very alone right now, but in terms of what you are feeling, you really are not alone.

Of those thousands of people going through a similar experience to you, some won't come out the other end too good at all; they'll lose sight of what it is they truly want and sink deeper into the depths of despair by allowing themselves to focus on what it is that they don't want. Others will come out the other end as a new person, embracing life in an all new way and ultimately finding a new partner. Others again will come out of it with their ex holding their hand in a relationship with the same person but that is much happier and joyful than it ever was before.

In all of these cases, the difference that separates those that win their ex back or find a new partner to enjoy life with, and those that don't, is one simple thing: the way you set yourself up to deal with the pain right from the beginning.

Let's be honest. The pain isn't going to go away any time soon. It just isn't. Don't expect it to. Neither does learning that there are other people going through the same thing dull the pain either. The pain you're feeling is yours and yours alone but that doesn't mean it will last forever either; it just feels like it will.

Mental pain is absolutely no different to physical pain. A wound is a wound and like all wounds it needs time to heal. A significant wound needs longer time. You wouldn't expect a broken arm to mend within a few minutes, now would you? A broken heart is no different. In fact, a broken heart can take a lot longer than a broken arm to mend and it can be just as painful, if not more! I'm sure, right at this moment of your life, you agree!

So what does it mean to "set yourself up to deal with the pain?" Think about the broken arm analogy. Do you think you'll help your broken arm heal if you don't hold it in place so that it can set straight? Do you think your body will heal it fast if you don't eat well and allow yourself to get sick? Do you think it will heal if you rob it of the nutrients it needs by drinking nothing but alcohol? Do you think it will heal if you keep using the arm and fail to rest it? Of course it won't.

The same goes for a broken heart. Like a broken harm, it will keep hurting for a while, but it will heal that much faster if you take care of yourself. Don't drink alcohol, don't binge on junk food, and just as you shouldn't use your broken arm while its healing, don't try to rekindle love with your ex tonight, tomorrow, or even next week. Let your heart have some time to heal - that's what the pain is telling you that you need to do and you should listen to it.

The key to dealing with the pain is to remind yourself that like any wound pain is normal. Don't dwell on it, don't focus on it, don't wallow in it, and don't act as if the pain is too much to bear. It isn't. You can bear it, just as thousands of people have done before you, are doing right now as you speak, and will do so in the future. It is crucial that you don't allow yourself to weaken by letting the pain control you. Would you let the pain of a broken arm control you? Of course not! Let the pain be. Accept it. Notice it if you have to. But remind yourself that it's ok to feel hurt, it's ok to feel painful, it's normal, and that it is just a part of the process of working through what has happened towards getting your ex back.

Above all else, no matter what, do not turn to any vice to overcome the pain. Alcohol and junk food doesn't work. It might provide a temporary escape, but the fact is both of these things will only make matters worse in the long term. Worse, emotions cloud your judgment but not nearly as much as alcohol does. If you drink even one drop of alcohol, then expect to lose your ex forever when, while inebriated, you make the biggest mistake of your life by contacting your ex, sending an email, or doing something that you'll completely regret next day and forever.

Right now, say out loud:

> *"For now I'm off the alcohol. I will not drink alcohol or binge on junk food. I will keep myself healthy and alert, because if I don't, I might end up doing something that I'll regret forever, and I cannot afford to be weak. I must stay strong and smart to get what I want; otherwise I'll get what I don't want."*

Repeat this statement over and over, or another similar if that works for you, to make sure that you establish a firm conviction that as long as you're feeling pain from your breakup, you won't drink any alcohol and risk making things worse. If you have any alcohol in the house right now, pour it down the sink and resolve not to purchase anymore until such time as you feel good about your life once again.

Do you really want your ex back?

If you really want your ex back, you can stay off the alcohol, right?

If you really want your ex back, you can avoid junk food for now, right?

If you really want your ex back, you're willing to take the time to learn the way to go about it, right?

If you really want your ex back, you're willing to change those things about yourself that hurt your relationship, right?

You should be answering "yes" to all of these questions. If you answered "no" or had a moment of hesitation on any of them, then you should think seriously about your steps from this point forward. Even if you did answer categorically with a "yes" to each question, it is very important that you get clear in your mind the idea that you really, truly do want your ex back in your life *and not just think that you do.*

You see, it is very easy to get caught in the trap of desiring your ex back solely because you've lost him or her and not because in your heart you believe they are "the one." After all, if you're going to face the pain of your breakup and spend the next weeks to months of your life undergoing personal transformation in an effort to win their heart back, you should make sure that *winning your ex back is truly what you want.*

Human beings have a tendency to want what they can't have. If you read dating guides they'll often explain how to make people attracted to you by acting as if you're unobtainable. The average person's closet is full of junk they bought that they didn't want but purchased anyway purely to own it. It sounds silly, but a desire for what we don't have is in our nature, and you need to recognize this before you set about doing what you must to win your ex back.

So what is it that you loved about your ex that makes you so miserable to have now lost it? What was it about your relationship that was so ideal, so perfect that you currently can't bear the thought of never experiencing it again? What were those things that the two of you did together, said together and shared together that you so desperately want back in your life?

Again, alone and among the quiet, sit down and write down with pen and paper the various things about your ex and the relationship you shared that you want back. Try to define them very clearly so that there's no question in your mind what those specific, tangible things are.

Then, on a separate piece of paper, write down all those things that you don't want back. What didn't you like? Did she have likes you absolutely couldn't stand, or mannerisms that frustrated you? Were there things you wished you could have shared but that she didn't want to, or that you didn't want to? What things did both of you put up with regarding the other, just to be civil? And what things caused constant arguments or fights because you both couldn't see eye to eye?

Hopefully your list of what you didn't like will be small, but if it isn't, you should examine what you write very carefully. Are the things you don't like more than balanced out by the things you did like? They say that "opposites attract" and while this may be true in a sexual or sensual sense in the beginning of a relationship while things are all exciting and new, the reality is the longevity of any relationship is highly dependent upon similarities of mannerisms, similarities of interests, the ability to easily talk to one another, and many shared interests.

Ask yourself; if you were to grow old and wrinkly with your ex would your relationship still be just as awesome as it was in the beginning? When you're both full of arthritis and can barely get off the couch, will you still both laugh and chat because you both think the same and share the same interests and views? If not, you should seriously contemplate whether or not your ex has actually done the right thing by you by leaving now, freeing you up to find someone who does match with you more closely.

Try to define what it is about your ex that you want back specifically. Are these things specific to your ex, or are they things you could get from anyone if you were in a relationship with them? What is it specifically about your ex that you feel no one else can give you? List all those things that you shared and all those that you didn't. Are there any deal breakers when you really think about it?

Do you want him or her back because you fear loneliness, because you're hurting, because you don't want someone else to have them instead of you, or some other reason that isn't really about the quality of your shared companionship?

Or do you want your ex back because you truly believe in your heart that they are "the one"?

The 'Onion Peel' method

Since it is very important to determine that your reasons for wanting your ex back are genuinely heartfelt and born of what the relationship offers rather than a fear of what losing it does, here's a technique that you can use to help you get clear. It's called the "Onion Peel" method and it is designed to help you peel away at your own beliefs and thoughts about your ex and what he or she offers your life so that you can find out whether or not you are deluding yourself, or whether or not your relationship really is the one that you think it is - and whether or not it is worth saving.

If, right now, you're thinking "Of course it's worth saving" I ask that you perform this exercise anyway. Your life now is filled with emotion and your judgment may be clouded, but even if it isn't and you know what you're doing, this exercise is great for unearthing many subconscious thoughts you have about your ex that perhaps you are not conscious of. It is not uncommon for people to do this exercise and suddenly realize the cause of their breakup was something they had never thought of before.

Again, using pen and paper and not a computer, sit down alone, with quiet, and where no one will interrupt you for the next hour or two.

Write this question down word for word:

> *Why do I want to be with [your ex's name]?*

Then, write down the first answer that comes to mind. Don't think about it, don't analyze it, don't question it, and don't ignore it. No matter how trivial your answer may seem, write it down immediately.

Then repeat, over and over again, until you get to a point where you have no more answers. Always write the question before you write each answer. Don't read your answers, just put the pen and paper away. Take a break for a few hours, even up to a day is ok. Then return and repeat this whole process again, even if you end up writing down the exact same answers.

While you follow this process you'll find that you'll spiral through a range of different emotions. You'll probably smile at one point, maybe even burst out laughing at the positive thoughts you'll be having about your ex, and then at others you'll feel crushed, start crying or even wailing uncontrollably. It is such a simple technique yet it is a very powerful one because the constant action of writing down the question and reaching into the depths of your mind for an answer is one that brings to the surface many memories, good and bad.

You can repeat this process numerous times, over hours, days, or even weeks.

What this does is it helps you to clarify all the things you truly like about your ex together with justifications for why you want to be with them. But, what typically happens the more you push for answers is this: you find out just how many true reasons you have *that are specific to your ex*. You may be able to find only a few reasons and begin to wonder why you feel so shattered by your ex leaving. You may find yourself saying things like, "I loved this about [ex's name]" and then suddenly find yourself writing "but I really hated this…" Many people perform this task only to find by the end of it they've defined their perfect partner *and it isn't their ex*!

For the most part, however, this exercise can be used to help brainstorm everything that you have in your mind about what makes your ex your ideal partner. By the end of it if you haven't argued yourself away from restoring your relationship, you'll have a fantastic list of everything you appreciate about your ex; keep it handy from this point forward.

If in the near future you get back with your ex you'll be able to use it to remind yourself regularly of all the things to show your ex appreciation for. If you don't get back with your ex, then you'll have the perfect list through which to identify those things that you want from a partner and thereby prevent yourself from jumping into another dead end relationship. In a very real sense, what you create by performing the "Onion Peel" is a complete awareness of what you want from your perfect partner.

Accepting blame from your ex can work in your favor

We've already discussed the idea that from this point forward you will not blame yourself or your ex for what has happened. Self punishment or directing guilt or blame towards your ex is unproductive and won't help you restore the fun, joy and love to your broken relationship.

However, I recognize that the suffering a breakup causes is often so intense that it is very, very difficult to stop falling into the trap of blame and guilt. It may be that you just can't help feeling guilty, that you can't help slapping yourself across the head for allowing your ex to get so let down by you that they left, or that you just can't stop pointing the finger.

Remind yourself by saying out loud:

> *It doesn't matter who or what caused the relationship to break. What matters is not what happened, but what is going to happen.*

But, what happens when your ex doesn't do the same thing? If your ex has laid the blame at your feet then accept the blame. Allow your ex to feel like he or she is being heard, that you're acknowledging the problem, and that you agree, therefore, that the solution is *with you.*

Can you see how accepting blame in this manner can actually help you move forward because it puts control over the root cause right in your own lap? If it was your entire fault, then it is up to you to solve the problem!

So if your ex wants to lay blame, you should readily accept it and happily so! Remember, it doesn't matter who is really at fault, but if by accepting blame you can take action that will help show your ex you care enough to make the matter an introspective one, then you can win your ex back simply by taking responsibility. This is a far better situation than if your ex says, "It's not you, it's me." In this latter case, it is up to you to use subtlety to "Onion Peel" your ex because "it's me" is often a nice way of saying, "I just don't like all those straws you've put on the camel's back".

If your ex thinks it was your fault your task is to address the accusation by agreeing. Accept what is said to you, admit you understand by reiterating what your ex has to say and then demonstrate your awareness by openly stating that you agree and you're going to make sure it never happens again.

Of course, don't do this right away. At this point in time we are still concentrating on your own personal transformation. If your ex has already said these things to you, then we'll deal with how to communicate your acceptance later in the book. For now, you must absolutely not contact your ex if you can avoid doing so. If you can't avoid seeing your ex, such as if you work with him or her or live with him or her then we'll also cover how to deal with that later in the book. For now, our focus is on you.

All you have to do, at this moment, is accept any blame that has been thrown your way as your opportunity to take control of the solution. When it comes time to communicate your acceptance, the way you'll do it will work as reverse psychology. When someone points the finger at another they anticipate a fight; they expect an argument. After all, it is in our human nature to defend ourselves. But, when your ex doesn't get that, he/she'll be surprised to say the least. Once the "fight" doesn't eventuate, your ex will unconsciously become more receptive to your next response and, again, we'll cover that shortly.

Either way, whether you're struggling not to lay blame upon yourself or whether your ex is throwing it at you without restriction, the best way to proceed is without harboring any thought of punishment or blame towards your ex. As long as you can take responsibility for the cause you have the power to take control of the solution.

There's nothing to be gained by punishing yourself. Instead, try to reward your ex by doing what it takes to raise their level of happiness. There's nothing to be gained by being hard on yourself and even less by being hard on your partner. It's not about who was wrong, or why. It's about taking ownership of the solution.

Chapter 3: The Path to Getting Your Ex Back

By now you should have taken the time to define what went wrong with your relationship, what you should have or could have done different to prevent it and what it is about your ex that makes you want them back so badly. If necessary, repeat all the exercises of the previous section to make sure that you're being completely honest with yourself and that embarking on the path to win back the heart of your ex is exactly the right thing to do because from this point forward, that's what you're going to do.

And remember, you MUST continue with a conviction to NOT touch a drop of alcohol, binge on junk food, or go out of your way to contact your ex just yet.

No quick fixes

The path to getting your ex back is methodical, but it isn't magical. Don't expect to be able to wave a wand like Harry Potter and watch your ex appear in a puff of smoke, all things healed and forgotten. This may be what you want to happen but that's not the way it will happen. If you read any guides that refer to "getting your ex back with magic" then toss them in the bin. If you really want your ex back you don't want fluffy magical ideas on your side, you want real, tangible and practical psychological tools combined with step by step processes to help you transform yourself into exactly the type of person that will have your ex clambering back to you.

Whereas magic might happen with the wave of a wand in the blink of a fictional eye, practical psychological tools and personal transformation takes time. You must accept that the path to restoring any relationship is a long one. Sometimes it is a path travelled fast but mostly it's not. Furthermore, the longer it takes to rekindle a new relationship with your ex the more solid that relationship will be. With that in mind it makes sense to aim to go slow, doesn't it?

Aim to go slow. Take small steps. Think of your past relationship as having been like a snowball that broke into pieces and melted. To create a new snowball you must start with an all new snowflake, find more snowflakes and then slowly over time roll them all together to create an all new fresh snowball - only this time it's going to be an even bigger and even stronger one than the last.

Say out loud:

There are no quick fixes. If I want my ex back and I want our new relationship to last, then I must be patient and take it slow. If I rush it, I'll ruin it.

Repeat this statement until it becomes second nature in your mind and you can say it without reading it.

A planned strategy of repair

If you are to win your ex back there are two things that you have to achieve. The first is that you must overcome the issues of the past that led to your breakup. The second is that you must sell the "new you" to your ex in a way that leaves your ex convinced that the person and issues they left behind are no longer a part of the package of being with you now or in the future.

Both of these things will take time. Not only is "time the great healer" but also the task of winning your ex back is one that requires thought, planning, and effort. You can't just approach the task of winning your ex back with hope, luck and haphazard attempts to attract your ex again. Instead, you have to see the task ahead of you as a road along which you will achieve certain things, piece by piece, bit by bit, day by day.

In the field of project management the achievement of little goals along the way to the major goal is referred to as achieving "milestones". From now on, you're going to keep your mind focused not so much on your end goal of winning your ex back, but all the little milestones that must be achieved along the way. If you keep your focus on your milestones then the end goal will be achieved naturally and easily. Consider every single milestone a smaller goal along the way to your ultimate goal of winning your ex back. They are incremental steps to help you get where you ultimately want to go.

We've already covered one aspect of overcoming the issues of the past and that is by taking responsibility for them. Even when your ex blames you and it's not your fault, you should accept the blame so that you can move forward instead of staying stuck in the past. We'll cover more on techniques to overcome the past later in the book.

For now, you need to separate these two things in your mind. Selling your "new self" to your ex *is completely separate* from overcoming the issues of the past. This is because the latter is actually achieved a lot more easily than you might think once you openly take responsibility for those issues. But selling the "new you" is a more difficult task for not only does it involve demonstrating to your ex that they're not going to get the very thing they left if they come back to you, but you've *actually got to change.*

Fortunately, the changes that you have to make are already clear. Each thing you have to do to change who you are and the behavior you exhibit is laid out bare for you in the list you created where you wrote down the things you should have done to have kept your ex in the first place. The personal transformation you need to demonstrate to your ex is as simple as demonstrating to your ex all the behaviors that you have already written down that *you should have done.* In other words, you're now going to start doing them. Let's call these new behaviors "the new you."

The New You

Before we go on, say this out loud:

To win the heart of my ex back I need to change, and there are two ways to do that. The first begins with me personally and has nothing to do with my ex. The second is to start behaving around my ex in accordance with the way I should have been behaving before my ex left me.

Sometimes our behaviors become so in-grained in our personality that changing becomes very difficult. We can genuinely desire change and put all our effort into doing so, yet before we know it we slip back into our old patterns. *This usually happens because we try to change too much too quickly thereby sabotaging our efforts to create new long-lasting habits.*

The trick to becoming the person that those items on your list suggest you should have been before your ex left is to start small. The path to the peak of any mountain is traversed step by step and that's exactly how you need to proceed to win your ex back - step by step.

It is here that you should take a cue from the toolkit of the professional salesperson. When attempting to close a sale, a professional salesperson knows they should never go for the close straight away. They risk alienating the customer and losing the sale if they do. Instead, they aim to highlight all the features and benefits of the product first, one by one, and gain a "yes" from the customer to acknowledge each benefit as they do it. Psychologically, the more times a customer says "yes" to a product the more likely it is that they'll say "yes" to actually buying it in the end. Top salespeople know this, so they work hard, stay patient and make every effort to get their customers to say "yes" many times before they say, "Would you like it gift wrapped?"

Of course, your problem is that your ex has left you and you aren't really in a position, at least just yet, to start gathering "yes's". If you do you're more likely to inspire your ex to reaffirm their position of "no." After all, the moment they left you they sent the message of "no" loud and clearly. If you try too early to start gathering your first "yes", you're more likely to gather a "no" - even if you say all the right things and make all the right moves.

For now, you want to give your ex some space. So, how can you possibly go about changing yourself in a way that will make your ex interested if you can't start demonstrating new behaviors and attitudes towards your ex right away?

The answer is actually quite simple:

You must first redesign your own life for the better before you start trying to demonstrate you can redesign your shared life for the better.

When you first met your ex and the light of romance sparked it did so for a reason. As an individual, you were both compelling to each other. You were both interesting to each other. Neither of you were thinking about "your shared lives". You were both thinking about each other, individually, personally. When you became all excited about your ex as a person, it was because of all those little things about your ex that you found attractive. In the beginning, the "relationship" didn't even exist. It was just all about them and them alone - the "shared" aspect, the "together" part, came later.

You need to go back to the drawing board and redesign those things about your life that will make you and your life interesting to your ex or, for that matter, to any potential partner. If you, as a person, offer attributes and qualities that are compelling to another person then it is those compelling attributes that ignite the spark of attraction.

Now, you've already accepted that the connection has been broken between you both. But since your ex is no longer around, all you have to work with to restore the connection, for now, is YOU. How can you possibly be compelling to another individual, your ex or otherwise, if you're not compelling to yourself? How can your life be interesting to anyone else if it first isn't interesting to you?

The last thing you want to do is to try and win your ex back by presenting the same old you with the same old issues. Why would your ex want to come back to you if there isn't something new and exciting to entice them? Why would they want to come back if you look the same, act the same, and indicate that all your ex will get is the very same thing they had - the very thing that made them leave in the first place?

Further, the act of transforming yourself into something your ex won't be able to resist takes time, it takes effort and it takes focus. The benefit, of course, is that your energy and efforts will be directed into something constructive instead of wallowing in the pain and misery that you are currently stuck with. Not only does this help you deal with the pain of your breakup more effectively, but it will help overshadow any "negative feel" that others will get when they're around you. You know what it's like when you spend time around someone who is depressed and miserable - it isn't fun. If people feel like it isn't any fun to be around you, what hope will you have of inspiring anyone, including your ex, to take an active interest in you and want to become a part of your life? The answer is none.

So the path is simple. You need to transform yourself for the better. To do that, there are only two areas that you need to focus on: your mental outlook and your physical appearance.

A mental transformation

Now, this guide isn't a guide to self-improvement, it's a guide to getting your ex back, so we're not going to devote another 300 pages to the various techniques that might help you follow a path of self-improvement. To do that, it is highly recommended that you head down to the local bookstore and buy a couple of books and guides on the subject of personal improvement. There are many to choose from but if you're unsure about which one to get simply ask the shopkeeper to tell you which are the best sellers and buy one or two of those. If you can't afford to invest in a few books on self-development head on over to the library and hire them for free. There's no reason you can't get a hold of exactly what you need to start rethinking yourself, whether you can or can't afford it.

Aside from taking it upon yourself to study some self improvement guides there is another surefire method that is guaranteed to lift your spirits, give you more energy and an improved outlook and definitely raise your level of happiness. It's also simple and requires no personal or introspective analysis at all but it will have an enormous impact on your own state of mind and in turn how you will be perceived by your ex and all those around you in the future. It is this:

Find a new interest or hobby and throw yourself at it.

It could be an interest in something you've always had but have never had a chance to actually do. It could be anything, from building model planes to bodybuilding, from Mixed Martial Arts (MMA) to white water rafting. It doesn't matter what it is, so long as it is something that you love to do and will be able to spend a lot of time doing.

Now, we did just mention white water rafting but of course such a hobby is expensive. Only choose what you can easily afford to do. Don't choose anything that is so costly that you'll only be able to participate in it for a few minutes every month. The idea of choosing a new hobby is that not only will you enjoy doing it and not only will it help lift your spirits but that it will successfully consume a lot of your time too. The distraction will help you deal with the pain of your breakup more readily by not allowing you to wallow in it and it will also raise your energy levels by getting you doing something that you like to do.

Preferably choose something you've always wanted to do but even a new interest is just as good so long as it is something that you can get motivated and passionate about. Choose more than one interest if you can. For example, you might take up jogging, start writing a fiction novel and join an indoor tennis club all at the same time. The more new activities and interests you have to find enjoyment in and distract you from feeling bad, the better!

Don't underestimate the power of a new interest to change your life. You might think that you will join a tennis club purely to play a few games of tennis here and there. But, while at the tennis club you might notice an advertisement on the board to join a competition team. Next you might play in a competition and establish all new friendships that you didn't have a few weeks before. Those friendships might lead to even more experiences with your tennis partners. One of your tennis buddies might own a business and be looking for a new employee and before you know it you have a new job too. Your new job, new sport, and new excitement for life might help shatter your ex's current view of you, or you might even meet a new partner in your new job, at your tennis club, or through your new friends!

You can never predict where immersing yourself in a new hobby will lead, but there is one thing that is for certain:

you will fill a gap in your life. When your ex left so too did a large chunk of how you spend your time. It is in this "missing time" that many people sit around, drink alcohol, eat ice cream, and lose themselves to the gap that their departed ex has left them. But if you fill that gap with other interests and/or other people, you will save yourself from falling into the trap of becoming lazy, unhealthy, depressed, and ultimately unattractive to your ex or anyone else you might know.

A physical transformation

In order to transform yourself mentally it is good to try and choose a hobby or interest that isn't just physical. Writing a book, becoming an artist, building models, or even registering in a course to study a new vocation are all good examples of choosing an interest that gets your brain ticking.

But it is equally important that you also choose an interest or hobby that is capable of transforming your body too. Human beings are mind-body machines; to become the best you can be you need to do something that is good for your mind and something that is good for your body.

Getting up and going for an hour walk at sunrise then spending an hour in the gymnasium in the evening is a good start, but those kinds of activities also leave your mind open to brooding on what has happened to you. Try to pick a physical activity that won't give you time to think such as a martial art, indoor cricket, volleyball, and so on. Activities that also require you to concentrate fully on the activity while you're participating in it are the best to distract your mind while also working wonders for your strength and fitness.

And don't stop there. A physical transformation isn't just about your body looks; it's about how you feel. If you've had a beard for ten years, shave it off. If you've shaved for ten years, grow a goatee. If you have long hair, cut it short. If you have a shaved head, grow your hair. Take all those old clothes you have and toss them out; replace them with new clothes that make you feel great. Buy new runners, a new wallet and a new watch. Change your deodorant and start using an all new after shave. Even change your toothpaste.

If you always pay by debit card, start paying in cash. If you normally drive everywhere, start walking to where you want to go. Always go up the elevator? Now go up the stairs. Do you like to wear black shirts? Start wearing white shirts. Do you like woolen socks? Start wearing cotton socks. Do you always watch TV at night? Read a book, play some music, or better yet, don't even stay at home at night anymore. Go out and find a new hobby to get into that replaces everything you used to do.

It will feel great and, eventually, your ex will notice you are different. When you next see him or her, they'll see the change instantly. They'll notice all the things that are different about you. They'll even notice that you smell different. With a multitude of subtle differences, they'll then have less trouble believing that *you have changed* when you tell them about different aspects of your new life, because the fact that *you have changed* will be obvious to them just by the way you appear.

And it won't be just that you are dressed differently, groomed differently, or look different. It will be that you *are different* because by changing up all the things you used to do you will have *become different.* Of course, I'm not suggesting you need to change who you are just because you've broken up with your ex. Everything you do should be something you enjoy. What I am saying is you should embrace everything that you like, and leave behind everything that hasn't worked for you. Become more of your good qualities, and less of your poor qualities. But above all else, fun is the keyword.

The comparison date

By the time you've added a few new interests to your life and have radically changed up how you spend your days, how you dress, how you smell, and where your attention is being placed, one or two weeks should have past. In this time you'll find yourself getting worried that the longer you wait, the less chance you'll have of getting back with your ex. You may even feel compelled to contact your ex, meet up, and show her just how much you've changed. After all, a couple of week does seem like a long time when you're worried if you'll lose your ex forever.

But you must continue to keep your distance for now.

We'll discuss how to manage the initial contact with your ex together with when and how it should occur later in the book. But for now we'll assume that you are able, for the most part at least, to avoid your ex. Remember, time is the biggest healer of all and the longer you can go without speaking to your ex the better at this point. It will be hard, but you must not break.

Say this out loud:

Time is the great healer. The longer I can wait before contacting [your ex's name], the better it will be for our chances of getting back together.

It is possible that your ex left you for someone else. You may be fretting that the longer you go without contacting your ex the greater the chance your ex's relationship with the new person in their life will become secure. But, the truth is, every relationship is always the best in the beginning. The closer to the beginning that you try to push your way back in, the less your ex will be interested in hearing from you or listening to anything you have to say. In fact, the more likely it will be that your ex reaffirms that they want the new person and not you. You must not put yourself in this position.

Further, if your ex left you because of other reasons and you're worrying that they may meet someone else in the meantime, once again, recognize that this is just a worry and nothing more. If your ex hasn't met anyone else then *they haven't met anyone else*. If they have, then you will be in the same position as if they had left you for someone else. In fact, often a person will leave their partner because they are already interested in someone else and plan to ignite the new relationship shortly after. If your ex left you for this reason, you will have no way of breaking his or her interest in the other person at this point so there's no point trying.

Take comfort from the fact that in most cases there is no one else. It is merely that the relationship wasn't working. Most people end up single for a period of time after a breakup. In some cases they jump into another relationship, but statistics are on your side here too. Nearly all rebound relationships fail very quickly and when they do it is usual for the person involved to choose to avoid the pain of another breakup by avoiding another relationship for a while. Many people choose to stay single at this point and do so indefinitely.

You may feel concerned about what could happen between your ex and a potential new partner, but "what could happen" is out of your hands. At least, for now, you will know that if your ex is with someone else, or does take an interest in someone else, you are better off leaving a little time so that the initial "honeymoon period" of that relationship has a chance to run its course. What can you do in the meantime?

Believe it or not, the best step for you to take, once you're ready, is to go on a new date with a completely different person.

"Wait, what?" I hear you say. "No way, I'm not interested in anyone else. I want to get my ex back, not meet someone new!"

It may strike you as being completely against what you're setting out to achieve, but going on a date with someone fresh is *exactly what you need to do.* But not just "a date", this is a "comparison date".

What do we mean by a "comparison date"? A comparison date is where you go out on the equivalent of a date with someone who you find interesting, or who finds you interesting, for the purpose of experiencing something new and having a good time. No, you're not seeking to compare your ex to the person you're going on a date with; rather, the comparison is about yourself. It is a chance for you to compare what life is like without your ex when you are with someone who you must give your full and complete attention to. It is a chance to experience something that you could not have experience while you were with your ex. It is also a chance to be distracted by someone else who you may find interesting or fun to be around.

You see, a date is completely unlike socializing with friends or family. It is a setting where two people can truly take an interest in getting to know each other unlike what can be achieved in any other setting. Dating is a lot of fun and it is also very exciting once you get over the nervousness of the initial meeting. The misconception is that a date means you must end up romantically involved with the person you're on the date with. But that doesn't have to be the case, and we'll get to why in a moment.

Remember, your ex may go on dates too and, just like your comparison date, it doesn't mean neither of you won't want the other back after the fact. In reality, often it can be jealousy over becoming aware that you've gone on a date that may prompt your ex to contact you and, as we'll see later, no matter the reason *it is always better* if your ex makes contact with you rather than the other way around.

Of course, jealousy is not why you're going to go on a date and in all likelihood you will probably choose not to tell your ex that you've gone on a date. Instead, this is your chance to find out more about yourself and experience being with another human being in a fun setting with no stress and no commitment. The way you do that is by organizing your date through an internet dating service.

You see, there are lots of people out there who like to go on dates purely for the fun of being with a new person. The beauty of finding a date via an internet dating site is that you can pick the person you might want to go on a date with up front by matching your interests. This ensures that you will end up spending time with someone you'll be able to have a chat with and not worry about uncomfortable silences.

Now, when you establish your initial contact, it's time to be honest. You must tell this person that you'd love to go on a date and have some fun, but that you just ended a long relationship and so you're not ready for any form of commitment. Be clear that *the reason you want to go on a date is because you just want to have some fun with someone new.* Explain that you are in that "rebound" stage and so you would definitely not be wanting to start a new relationship, but that the person you are talking to is really interesting and it sounds like you'd get along, so you'd like to meet up just the same. It's as simple as explaining all of that throughout your conversation with this new person, and then saying, "You know what? Would you like to have a coffee sometime, no strings attached?"

If you've been clear about your situation and the person you're chatting to says, "Yes" then that's great! Now you can go on a "comparison date" without any guilt and without any intention other than to spend time with someone new who shares a few interests with you. The comparison between how you feel on your date and how you feel about getting back with your ex will help you get your head straight about where you want to go from there with total honesty.

Yes, in some cases you'll find the person you go on the date with may even be a better match for you than your ex. But of course, that's a good thing! But you will also find that by being open and honest about your situation you'll end up having a great time with a new friend who you may or may not have a coffee with again. If, of course, the date isn't so much fun, then that is a great comparison too!

Now, if you're sitting there thinking, "I can't do that, I can't go on a date" it is highly recommended that you jump on the internet, float on over to a dating site, and just sign up. Most are free and will give you plenty of opportunity to chat with other people. Your ex left you, remember, so there's no guilt about chatting with other interesting people. I guarantee that it won't take long before someone catches your interest and before, after you chat with them for a while, you'll find yourself compelled to keep the chat going, whether it is on the internet or in person. Once you do take a leap of faith and meet up in person, you'll gain a whole new perspective on your life. It will either propel you with even more passion and awareness back towards your ex, or it will help you gain perspective over what you truly want in life.

Chapter 4: The Right Kind of Perspective

A comparison date is a great way to have a lot of fun and is definitely a key tool to gain perspective on yourself, your ex, and what you want going forward. When combined with the amount of time you'll be dedicating to your new hobbies and interests, you'll find that even though you haven't actively made a move towards your ex just yet, you'll be well on the way to appearing completely different to your ex once you do.

Throughout all of the changes you've been making in your life, and all of the new people that those changes have allowed you to interact with, you'll find that your awareness about yourself, your ex, and what you want out of life will have grown quite substantially. You may still be feeling terrible at the loss of your ex, but you'll also find that the more you do of what has been discussed so far, the more you'll be viewing getting back with your ex as a great positive step instead of a way to overcome a severely negative situation.

This is the right kind of perspective to have.

When most people suffer a devastating breakup their follow-up actions are often born from a motivation to move away from the pain the breakup has caused. Fear of loneliness and desperation not to lose a loved one are the worst kinds of perspectives upon which to base a rekindled relationship. The strength in a relationship is derived through the constructive and positive qualities that allowed the relationship to flourish in the first place. If you want your ex back and you want it to last once they come back, then you have no other choice but to build a positive, constructive foundation for it.

The more you can groom yourself to think positive thoughts towards your ex, the greater will be your chance of attracting your ex back. It is literally impossible to think positively or constructively when you're wallowing in misery, allowing yourself to fall into depression, and failing to distract yourself with other people and other interests while your ex is gone. But as long as you add new purpose to your life in the form of new interests and activities, purposefully embark on a course of self-improvement and introspection, and invigorate yourself with a change of appearance as well as a change of scenery, your ability to maintain a healthy perspective will be that much stronger.

Make it your mission to remain conscious of everything you do, say, or think. Everything you do from this point forward must be easily checked off against the following question:

Is this constructive?

Positive thinking is a way of putting a shine on things *but* constructive thinking is a way of turning things into shine. Do you see the difference? We can't always think positively because sometimes things "just plain suck" and when they do it's hard not to feel bad about them. But the truth is there's nothing wrong with feeling frustrated, there's nothing wrong with feeling bad, and there's nothing wrong with having negative thoughts about anything at all. The problems begin only when the thoughts and actions you have become something you dwell upon and/or when they become destructive.

So don't dwell on them. Don't allow them to become destructive to your life. With everything you think, say or do, ask yourself:

Is this constructive?
If it isn't, ask yourself:

How can I turn this into something constructive?
For example, imagine you are sitting at home, alone, and a song comes on the radio that reminds you of your ex. As you listen, you become depressed and upset, perhaps even crying. The lyrics in the song remind you of everything you've lost. As you're listening, ask yourself: Is listening to this song constructive? You'll know instantly that it isn't because it is making you feel sad, making you depressed, and overall making you feel bad. Next, ask: How can I turn this into something constructive? You might immediately think the answer is to switch the radio off, or put on some more enjoyable music (perhaps soundtrack action music that has no lyrics!), or perhaps you'll start saying to yourself, "Well, I used to love this song. I remember when I did love it, I used to do this and that" and thus you start to associate different more positive memories to the song.

When you begin to change many different aspects of your life, and once you get the hang of converting any situation into something constructive the moment you become aware that it has become destructive, your perspective will broaden greatly. Not only that, but you'll find yourself imbued with a much more pleasant and positive personality and *it is precisely this kind of an outlook that will make you more attractive.*

The art of listening

Of course, changing all of these elements of your life won't happen overnight. In fact, many of the changes that you'll start making won't completely realize themselves before you see or contact your ex next. Remember, there are no quick fixes and while some things will click for you overnight, just as many won't.

If you have no way of avoiding your ex in the meantime, or if a few weeks have passed and you feel you are now ready to make contact again, there is one thing above all else that will help you broaden your perspective and come across as being more pleasant and likeable that you can put to work in your favor straight away, and it is this:

The ability and willingness to actively listen.

Each time that you speak with your ex it is likely that he or she will have something to say about you, about the relationship, about their own life, about where you both once were and where things are going. It may be what you want to hear, it may not be what you want to hear. It may be unpleasant, or it may be great news. But one way or the other, your ex will have something to say.

So listen. Really listen. Don't just hear. Don't just let the words go in your ears while your mind is ticking over with what you're going to say next. One of the great keys to effective communication is to take the time to pause in between the end of what one person says and the beginning of what you say. Such a pause appears courteous, but at the same time it is a moment in which you can think about how you want to craft your response.

Practice the art of listening using everyone around you *before* you try to listen closely to your ex. Get used to noticing the subtle facial movements, the tone of voice and the body language behind everything being said to you. Listening isn't just about hearing words; it's about detecting all the subtle nuances in the message coming your way. Listen carefully not just with your ears, but with your whole being. Make an effort to consider everything from the perspective of the person you're conversing with. Master this, and when it comes time to talking to your ex, he/she will be amazed at just how attentive to them you've now become.

The best thing about listening correctly is that it gives you a greater awareness and understanding for what the person, or your ex, is trying to say to you. Greater awareness gives you exactly the kind of perspective you need to be able to answer with exactly what the person wants or needs to hear. Remember, you can't fake listening attentively; your response will be a dead giveaway, each and every time. The last thing you want is for your ex to think you're not listening to their needs, so at no point give them this feeling. Listen attentively, don't interrupt, pause before replying and use your pause to carefully craft your response - and then respond.

Listening in itself can be the make or break of getting back with your ex, so above all else make it your mission to break any old interrupting habits, or any old narcissist tendencies, and give your whole attention to whoever you talk to. Especially do so to your ex.

Chapter 5: The Big 'Three' No-No's

Whether you're in contact with your ex every day or whether you contact him/her many weeks after your breakup and after you've implemented major changes to your life, there are three things that remain absolutely crucial that YOU MUST NOT DO if you are to break through the barrier that currently separates you. These are:

- Don't reek of desperation
- Don't cling to your ex
- Don't try to exert control

Don't reek of desperation

The key to not appearing desperate is calm intention

Let's be honest, right about now you're feeling pretty desperate. You're desperate not to lose your ex forever. You're desperate to take action to prevent yourself from being lonely. You're desperate to overcome the pain you are feeling. You're desperate to make amends. You're desperate to right what has gone wrong. You're desperate to rekindle the loving, perfect relationship that you've lost.

The first thing you need to do is acknowledge to yourself with honesty that *you really are desperate.* You must make sure that you don't fall into the trap of saying, "I'm not desperate" only to find yourself doing and saying things that reek of desperation. The first step to doing that is to acknowledge that you are, in fact, feeling desperate.

Say this out loud:

I know that I'm desperate to win [your ex's name] back BUT I'm not going to allow myself to show it.

You see, the key to not appearing desperate is to always, at all times, remain calm, and one of the best ways to remain calm is to *pretend to be calm.* It sounds odd but many people who you see that you think are cool, that you think are calm, that you think are very collected and purposeful with their actions, are people with emotional issues and flaws just like everyone else. However, they've managed to keep their inner turmoil hidden from view and *they do it by presenting what they want you to see.*

The key to presenting yourself as a calm and methodical person is to start by pretending to be that which you want to be. Through pretending, a kind of acting, you can deliberately present the type of person that you want others to see. And it's actually easier than you can imagine. Don't set out to become a 100% calm and collected person 24/7 from day one. Instead, prepare yourself before you allow yourself into a situation that could turn emotional. Resolve that if you start feeling emotional that you will try to stay calm for just 10 seconds. Take a deep breath, hold it and then exhale while counting to 10. You can stay calm for ten seconds, right? Well it's as simple as doing that, and then doing it again and again and again. There's no such thing as being calm forever but you can be calm for a few seconds, and a few more, and a few more, right when it counts.

Practice being calm by counting to ten and breathing with intention, and you'll find that even when you can't stop feeling desperation you'll be able to make yourself appear as if you're not desperate at all. Appearances are everything, but of course, the beauty of calming yourself for 10 seconds at a time is that, after a while, it becomes a very natural thing to do. Before you know it calm will become a habit and, when it does, any feeling of desperation will be gone, replaced by a feeling of calm intention.

Say this out loud:

> *By training myself to be calm for 10 seconds at a time I can eliminate all feelings of desperation and ultimately replace them with feelings of intention.*

Repeat this statement a few times and as you do notice how much more powerful it is to think "I intend to get my ex back" than it is to think "I have to get my ex back." Intention, instead of desperation, is a much more powerful state of mind.

The 'urgent, 'important, and 'guilt' mistakes

Desperation has a way of making itself known in three very obvious but harmful ways. It will plead to get what it wants, it will put pressure on to get what it wants, and it will try to make you feel bad if you don't listen. Even as you begin to establish a feeling of calm intention towards getting your ex back, you must remain mindful of these three ways in which desperation will try to get its way because if you're not, these three ways will harm your chances of getting back with your ex. Be mindful to notice them and as you do pause, breathe, count to 10 and stop them in their tracks. Let's take a look at them now.

Desperation mistake #1: Pleading and begging

Never say, "Please come back to me" or "You have to give me a chance." Any form of begging or pleading is perceived as desperation.

Desperation mistake #2: Claiming it's important

Don't leave messages on your ex's answering machine like, "You have to call me back, it's urgent" or "It's important we talk, call me as soon as you can" or "Please, please, please call me soon." Remember, your ex left you and when they did they made the decision that you are no longer important to their life. By claiming otherwise, you'll only force their defense mechanisms into action. No matter how important you think something is, you have to remind yourself that claiming such will make you appear desperate.

Desperation mistake #3: Putting on the guilt.

An absolute no-no is to contact your ex and say, "I just can't live without you" or "Don't ruin everything" or "You've made my life a misery" or "If you don't call I don't know what I might do". We've already discussed how blame and punishment must be put out of your perspective and guilt is just one form of punishment. Don't give your ex any reason to think that you are trying or intending to make them feel guilty for anything, at all.

Don't cling to your ex

The key to not appear as if you're still clinging

We've already discussed the importance of accepting your situation. By now you should have taken the time to remind yourself that your ex is gone and that you don't even want back what you've lost; what you want is your ex back in an all new, all fresh relationship.

If you've been taking the advice given so far, then unless you are completely unable to avoid your ex on a daily basis, you should not contact them either. Appearing as if you're "clinging" should therefore not be an issue for you.

Many people ruin the potential they have to rekindle their relationship by refusing to let go. When they refuse to let go, they're on the phone every ten seconds trying to get their ex to talk to them. They go around to his or her home, they rock up to their workplace, and they send an email every day or even every five minutes. They are there, constantly, in their ex's face, day after day, week after week.

All you have to do to not appear as if you're clinging to your ex is to sever contact for a short period of time. It is really that simple. If you can't avoid your ex on a daily basis, that's ok. He or she won't think you're clinging if they know that you have to be near them because you work together, live together, play sport together, have related friends and so forth. But, when you are near each other because being so is unavoidable, you must make it your mission to give them space. That doesn't mean you should ignore them; what it means is that you should acknowledge them but allow them to be as free of you as anyone else in the room, in the workplace, and so forth.

For the first few weeks of your breakup, you must absolutely give your ex complete freedom to experience life without you. If you don't, you may risk being perceived as clinging on and, since your ex left you so that you wouldn't be a prominent feature of their life, you'll damage their perception of you if you don't allow them to get what they wanted.

Remember, until you can accept it's over, until you can stop trying to micro-manage your ex back into your life, until you can stop forcing your way in through fear of losing your ex forever, you will lose your ex. Accept the situation that you are now single, and keep working towards making the changes that will bring your ex back naturally. Clinging is forcing and it will work against you. Remind yourself of this at all times.

Stop trying to control the situation

The key to showing you're in control

Reeking of desperation and clinging to your ex are loud and clear signals that you're out of control. They are alert beacons to your ex that you can't let go and, since they left you, that will be *the last thing they want*. Next you'll find your ex trying to get even more space from you and, if you are still desperate and clinging, their action will only prompt you to become even more desperate and clinging.

You must break this vicious cycle by allowing your ex to do what they want, be who they want, go where they want, date who they want, say what they want, and experience whatever they want - without you. Yes, this feels like you're losing control over your ex, but in reality giving your ex complete freedom just as they want is in fact *gaining control over them.*

We've already discussed the notion that you must take responsibility for the situation - that if your ex blames you for their decision to leave, that you will accept this as it is the ideal way in which you can take control over the solution. Recognize that "control" and "force" are two independent things. You don't want to force anything and you don't need to force anything to gain control. In fact, the most powerful forms of control are those where people have absolutely no idea that you are exerting control over them. You can control how well your ex responds to you by giving them the freedom they desire, and you can lose control over their response by not giving them that freedom.

Remind yourself that everything that is occurring is short term. The odds of losing your ex forever diminishes the more freedom you give them in the short term. The less freedom you give them, the higher the odds that you'll lose them forever.

The key to showing that you're in control is to stop trying to control. When you combine your intention to give your ex the freedom they crave with your calm and controlled approach to eliminating all acts of desperation, your ex won't give a second thought to whether or not you are forcing any issues.

Chapter 6: Contact Strategies

Up until this point we've devoted considerable time to laying the foundation that will support you once you take direct action towards winning your ex back. Everything so far has been about crossing the "t's" and dotting the "i's" to ensure that all future interaction with your ex will be positive, constructive, and framed in a way that will increase the odds that your ex will move towards you rather than further away from you.

Make sure that you follow - and continue to follow - all of the advice so far. Don't underestimate the importance of anything included in this guide for to do so would be to take a risk with rekindling your relationship that simply isn't worth taking. Everything, no matter how minor it may appear to you on a surface level, is of high value to the end goal of winning your ex back and the ongoing goal of keeping him or her forever.

If you haven't seen or heard from your ex in many weeks take heart in the knowledge that everything you've done so far has been a step on the path to winning your ex back. Now, however, it is time to take the step of actually making contact.

The ideal time to contact

There are different schools of thought about what timeframe constitutes the ideal distance between when your ex leaves and when contact should be made. Some people recommend two weeks, others a few days, and others again suggest no earlier than one month. Ignore them all. There is only one truth about the ideal time to contact your ex and *that is when you feel like you've given them enough space and, if required, could continue to give them more.*

Naturally this is not to suggest you should contact them after just a few days because you would know in your heart that such a short time frame is by no measure "enough space." Giving your ex enough space to feel free of you involves allowing enough time to heal some of the negative thoughts your ex had about you that led him or her to leave. In other words, enough time should have passed that some of the negative feelings your ex will have had about you will have diminished somewhat.

Unfortunately, you are unable to judge exactly how long this will be, but at the same time no text book can tell you either. The nature of your ex's thoughts about you, and how negative they are, will in some part be determined by how smoothly your breakup went, why they felt the need to leave in the first place, how long such thoughts have been festering in their mind, and a whole host of other issues that can never be made black and white. If you give a few weeks to a month of space this is generally a good ballpark to work around, however it should not be made a rigid timeframe. The only rigidity that you should apply is to yourself.

The rule is this: don't contact your ex if you're feeling desperate to do so.

As long as you're feeling desperate to do so then you have not allowed enough time to get your head on straight. Further, you have not allowed enough time, nor taken enough action, to get yourself to a state where you will be so well focused on your own life that it will become compelling to your ex. As long as you're desperate you're primary focus is towards your ex's life and as we've already discussed such a focus is likely to lead you to think, say and do all the wrong things that will harm rather than help your cause.

After you've spent time re-inventing yourself, immersing yourself in new hobbies and interests, perhaps had one or more comparison dates, and spent time getting clear while avoiding alcohol and junk food, a few weeks at the very least should have past. If you want to contact your ex, just ask yourself: will I be ok if I don't contact him/her? If the answer is yes, then you're probably ready to make first contact.

There is also another way that allows you to be sure that you're ready and that is, after weeks of changing up your life, if you wake up and don't think about your ex at all. If the day is rolling along happily and half way through or towards the end you realize you hadn't thought about them at all, then you're ready.

The exception to everything stated so far is if you are unable to avoid your ex on a daily basis due to other related or connected commitments that you both have, such as sharing a workplace. In this instance, you've technically already made your first contact because you can't avoid it. However, if you've been following the guidance so far you will have continued to give your ex the personal space he/she needs, and so your real "first contact" scenario will be the same as if you had not been seeing or interacting with your ex at all.

The ideal method of contact

When contacting your ex for the first time after a break never use the telephone. Don't rock up to their workplace to meet them personally. Don't knock on their parents' door and ask to see them. Don't hang about the gym they frequent and don't buzz them using Skype. In other words, your first contact *must not* occur in person or verbally. Whether you've been unable to avoid your ex or whether you haven't seen him/her for weeks, your first method of contact must be in writing.

If your first thought is to open an email client and bang away a letter, forget it. Forget typing an instant message and absolutely do not use Twitter. Not only must your first contact avoid being in person or becoming a verbal conversation, you must also avoid anything that is potentially *real* time or that is ordinary. Twitter conversations occur in real time. Email can occur in real time, but even when both parties aren't sitting at their PC's, emails are very common to send and receive, so email communication is "ordinary." There is only one way that you can communicate with your ex that is out of the ordinary, that isn't in real time, and that can't be ignored with a delete button, and that is to go old school with a handwritten letter.

Handwritten letters offer many advantages. They are a very tangible, touchy-feely type of communication that can evoke more impact than an ordinary, every-day method of communication like email. They are also something that can be read in an uncommon place. Whereas your ex may be used to reading emails at her desk, they will be able to take your handwritten note to a quiet area of the park.

Emails are more likely to be forgotten, but a handwritten note can be left in a man's pocket, in a woman's purse, on the dresser, on the coffee table, and so on. In fact, it is very common for people to read a handwritten note and then re-read it again and again across a wide range of different locations. There is an unconscious benefit to this. Whenever someone reads a handwritten note in an uncommon location it is because they aren't doing anything else. If they're waiting for a tram, it helps them pass the time. If they are sitting in the park, it is because they are taking a break. If it's at the coffee shop, it's because they want to read your note while sipping on their latte. The beauty of this fact makes a handwritten note impossible to interrupt them when they don't want to be interrupted - a crucial ingredient of first contact success. Or, to put it another way, a handwritten note is more welcomed into the life of the person receiving it than any other form of communication - and that subconscious "welcome" feeling is then extended to you as the sender of the note.

Finally, don't drop the note in a letter box. Don't secretly slide it onto your ex's desk. Don't use any clandestine method at all to deliver it. Mail it the old fashion way - envelope, stamp and all. There is another good reason for doing this. By allowing your handwritten note to arrive by snail mail, it is a demonstration that you are not out of control. It doesn't reek of desperation because snail mail actively demonstrates patience!

What to say in your initial contact

Here are the basic principles to apply to your handwritten note:

- It must not attempt to set up a meeting time
- It must not make your ex think you want a reply
- It must not give any indication that you want your ex back
- It must be written in a pleasant, friendly, neutral tone

- It must be very, very short
- It must be 90% about you, and 10% about your ex
- The 10% about your ex must make them feel good
- The 90% must make them feel good about you
- It must directly shift responsibility for everything to you
- It must categorically confirm the relationship is over
- It must convey that something good has happened to you

The very first time you contact your ex your mission is simple. You want to eradicate all ill feelings towards you that led to your breakup and that may have arisen during the course of your breaking up BUT at the same time you must evoke a sense of curiosity in your ex about what you're doing with your life now that they are gone. Make no mistake. There are very few breakups in which the partner that chose to leave the relationship doesn't wonder what their ex is up to, who they are seeing, how they are feeling, and what impact they've had on their life by leaving. *Everyone wonders.* You have to add to this wonder by suggesting that things for you have taken a turn for the better. You have to make them think that losing you wasn't the end of your world; it was the beginning. You have to make them think that the perception they had of you is now wrong because, for a reason they can't pinpoint, you're different. *They'll wonder why and the more they wonder the more they'll want to know the answer.*

Let's now take a closer look at the keys to making this work by expanding upon each of the above bullet points, one by one.

Don't set up a meeting time

The moment your ex realizes the handwritten note is from you they'll be expecting to see your desperation oozing through, usually with an expectation that you'll ask to meet up. They'll be waiting for the "call me please". They'll be looking for the inevitable, "Can't we just try again?" plead. In other words, in some way shape or form, they'll be expecting you to suggest that they meet up or contact you and that you both get back together.

The moment you fail to meet that expectation you shatter one illusion they have about you. The pre-conception that you're desperate, controlling, or trying to force any issue will begin to break down. They'll begin to wonder why and this wonder acts like a seed that will rapidly grow into a genuine desire to actually contact you and find out.

You don't want a reply

Remember earlier we mentioned that the more human beings don't have something the more they want it? There are many ways you can use this principle of behavior to your advantage and one such way is to actively state that your ex doesn't have to reply. Of course, you don't want to say *don't reply* because the truth is you really want your ex to reply as soon as they can of their own volition! So, instead, say something like this:

"I don't expect to hear from you and that's ok, I just wanted you to know that as far as I'm concerned, we're all good."

The more times you convey the message that you don't expect a reply from your ex, the more your ex will feel a lack of pressure to reply. But, as your lack of pressuring for a reply continues, your ex will feel pressure building to find out why you aren't pressuring. It's a snowball effect that will, in due course, have your ex busting at the seams to know why.

You don't want your ex back

You must never, at any point, hint that you want your ex back. Conversely, you must never say that you don't want them back (the previous principle does not apply here!). Your ex left you for one or more reasons and at this point you can't be sure how withered those reasons have become. For all you know those reasons have become stronger with time (though doubtful). Either way, you have to assume that the reasons you ex has in his/her mind for why they left remain intact, and so for this reason you must not directly or indirectly state or hint that you want them back. Doing so is sure to further reinforce those reasons because the moment your ex thinks you want them back they'll immediately think of the reasons why they left.

Never give your ex a reason to think about why they left. Never give them a reason to question whether or not they should honor anything you want. Your mission is to make your ex think that you will honor everything they want.

Write in a friendly, pleasant tone

An angry, hurt, frustrated, scared, desperate, controlling, forceful, rushed, abrupt, or uncaring tone is sure to reinforce to your ex that you are everything they don't want in their life. The opposite is true. The most attractive person in the world isn't just attractive because of their looks or their physique, it is *who they are* that makes or breaks how attractive they are perceived. That's why the "funny guy' who is also supremely fat and ugly can still get the girl!

A warm and friendly tone is simply more attractive than any other. But more than that, your ex will be expecting you to contact them at some point, even if by accident in the street. In their mind they'll have built up a pre-conception about how you'll be: sad, angry, depressed, confused, etc. But by portraying yourself as happy, friendly, warm, caring, and most of all level-headed, you'll be demonstrating once again that you aren't the person they think you are. You'll also be demonstrating that, once again, something about you has changed. Your ex will begin to wonder why you sound so warm and happy. They may even begin to think you may have met someone else. Don't worry, this is a good thing! The more your ex wonders why you are this "new way" the more he/she will be compelled to find out and establish direct contact.

Keep your letter short

A long letter explains too much, says too much, gives away too much, reduces the mystery, and may inadvertently seal your fate when you say too much about something you should have said nothing about. Keep your letter short. Stick to the game-plan. Only say what needs to be said, and we'll cover that shortly.

Keep it 90% focused on you, 10% on your ex

The last thing you want to do is appear like you're a narcissist in your contact, especially if one of the reasons your ex left is that you didn't show them enough attention! However, you also don't want to trip yourself up by talking too much about your ex either, for to do so would betray a sense of desperation, a sense of loss, and that your mind is firmly on your ex and not only our own life (something that flies in the face of the principle of making your life compelling to your ex once again).

By "90% on you" I don't mean to spend 90% of your note talking about what you are up to, how you've changed, or anything like that. Your note will be too short for such detail anyway. Instead, the 90% is about how you think and feel about where things are at and about why you have sent the note. It's not "about you" as much as it's "your perspective on the situation."

The "10% on your ex" is technically also about your perspective. It is that part of the letter where you say, "I hope you are doing well, I know you made your decision for the right reasons and I'll always support you in whatever you do." Remember, your entire letter must make your ex feel good. You must agree with them, accept responsibility for anything they blame you for, and you must acknowledge and accept their decision.

"I will always respect you utterly and support your decisions completely."

Taking complete responsibility

You won't want to focus on this aspect in your letter but you will want to demonstrate that you accept you were responsible for what happened and that you are deeply sorry about it. Don't make a specific or direct announcement. Include it in your "it's time to move on" statement, as shown below.

It's time to move on

The last thing you want is to let your relationship just disappear and move on. But it's the first thing you want your ex to think you're prepared to do. What do you think happens when someone feels like they've had enough of you? They want to get away and have as little of you as possible. But what do you think happens when a person feels like they've gotten away, that they now have as little of you as possible and that you're now a better person than they thought you were? That's when they stop thinking about getting away. Once they do that, they become more receptive to listening to what you have to say. It is from here that progress is made.

Fail to make them think they can get away from you if they want and they'll be compelled to get away from you just to prove they can, even if in their heart they don't really want to. Don't break the cardinal rule of seeming like you are trying to control your ex. Allowing them to think you agree everyone can move on will hand control back to them. Your first handwritten note is about acknowledgment and about demonstrating acceptance of the situation. It's where you say:

"I know you're right, I made those mistakes and you're right to say 'enough'. I don't blame you at all, I just made mistakes. I should have helped make us stronger and not have done anything to harm what we had. But time goes forward, not back, so all I can do now is respect your decision and move on with my life too. I just want you to know I have nothing but good memories of you and I wish nothing but the best for you, forever."

Something 'good' has happened

If there is anything about your initial contact that is the backbone of your whole approach, it is this: to indirectly convince your ex that something good has happened to you. It is this "mystery thing" that will have your ex thinking constantly about you and it is this unknown "new thing in your life" that will compel them to want to talk to you fast.

Your task is to convince your ex that something about your life has changed for the better. Hopefully this won't be hard because if you've been following the advice so far *something should have changed for the better.* You should have a new hobby or more, have met new people, and feel good about a great number of changes you've been making to your grooming, your dress, your environment, your outlook, and so forth.

But whether or not you truly feel good about change or not is largely irrelevant. You must make your ex think you feel good about it. Do this by dropping a single, subtle, but clear line:

"I must admit, I thought it would be impossible to enjoy life without you. But things have changed so fast that I can now see why you thought we'd be better off if we went our separate ways."

Can you see how with a statement like this you haven't mentioned anything specifically that is "better without your ex" but you've certainly hinted something is. Your ex will automatically assume you've met someone else and, if not, will wonder what exactly "changed so fast" to make you think positive of the fact that they left you.

The moment your ex left he/she made the decision that they'd be better off with you. But the moment they believe you agree with that decision, they'll want to know why. It is in their desire to find out more that they open themselves to learning more about the new you and your new life. Only with that door open can your ex eventually walk back into your life.

The 'my time with you was the best' approach

At this point you may be feeling a little confused or disjointed about the whole process of getting your ex back. After all, up until this point a great deal of this guide has focused on accepting your ex is gone, changing your life, going on dates with other people, and now writing to your ex to say you accept it is over and that you're moving on. How can any of that help? All of it helps, but granted, there is one slight danger in taking such an approach.

If you slip up even slightly you run the risk of inadvertently communicating to your ex that not only are you accepting that they are gone, but that you are glad they have gone. Suggesting you are "better off without them" as per the previous example may infer the wrong message. To make sure it doesn't, you need to counter balance it and the best way to do that is to emphasize that no matter how your life is now, you'll always consider your time with your ex to have been the best time of your life.

Now, the risk of counter-balancing is that if you go too far you can undo all the progress you've made in convincing your ex that you're over them and able to move on. So here's how you must say it:

"No matter what happens from here, I want you to know that my memories of you will always be the best. I'll always think of what we had as awesome, and consider the stuff that went wrong as mistakes that should have been avoided

but weren't. When I put all the mistakes I made out of my mind, our time together is something I never want to forget."

Can you see how this statement achieves a number of things: it shows you are accepting the mistakes in the relationship were yours, that you think your ex is awesome, that you think highly of them, that they were right to leave, that you hold no grudge, you have no blame, and most of all that had you not made the mistakes the relationship was "the best". Further, the statement "no matter what happens from here" is a subtle way of saying, "you can leave me if you want, but you can come back to me too if you want, no pressure."

Don't give your ex the impression that you want the relationship back. Don't give your ex the impression that you're "happy" that the relationship ended. Take the neutral approach but with a warm, responsibility accepting tone. And always reinforce how good the relationship was and that you'll never forget it (another way of saying, I'm good to move on but I know I'm losing something great).

The difficulty with convincing your ex that you are ready to move on is that you can inadvertently give your ex the impression that the reason you are comfortable to let things slide is that the relationship was never that good in the first place. So say something like:

"I know I blew it, but that won't stop me from regarding what we had as something that should have been preserved and kept forever. My mistake, my bad, my regret, but that's ok; I won't dwell on it because the past is the past. I'll just think about the good times when I remember us, because even though I screwed up, I don't have to let it ruin the

memories of the good things we had and I hope in time you won't either."
Whatever you do say, make sure you do so in your own words but keeping all of these principles in mind.

Here is an example first contact letter:

Hi Jane,

You may not want to hear from me so I'll keep this short. I just wanted you to know a few things.

First, you were right. I made mistakes that should never have been made and when I think about the impact of those on what we had I see exactly why you felt like it was time to leave. I apologize to you for that as you certainly didn't deserve anything but the best from me.

I also wish to apologize for the way I behaved when you last saw me. I was worried how life would be without you and that's one reason why I behaved so poorly. But having time to gain perspective, and with things changing so fast so quickly, I can now see why you thought we'd be better off if we went our separate ways. You know in my heart I only want the best for you, so I truly hope you get the best now and in the future.

I know I blew it, but that won't stop me from regarding what we had as something that should have been preserved and kept forever. My mistake. My bad. My regret. I'm not ok with how I made you feel, but I am now ok with your decision to move on. But I want you to know that from here on I'm only going to think about the good times when I remember us, because even though I screwed up, I don't have to let it ruin the memories of the good things we had.

Well my short letter is already getting long so I'll leave it there. Just know that no matter what happens from here, my memories of you will always be the best. I'll always think of what we had as awesome, and consider the stuff that went wrong as mistakes that should have been avoided but weren't. When I put all the mistakes I made out of my mind, my time with you was something I never want to forget.

Love always and your friend forever,

John

How to get your ex to return your messages

If you apply the strategy above in all likelihood your ex will feel compelled to return contact. It is doubtful that he/she will send a handwritten note, and more likely that they'll either find a way to meet personally, send an email, or pick up the phone - probably the latter. The reason for this is they will have questions that they know they may not get an answer to if they don't ask you directly.

However, it is also possible that your initial contact letter won't get a response. This is the least likely scenario but, depending on the nature of your breakup, still possible. If you don't get a reply, don't worry. Remember, the intention of your letter wasn't to get a reply but to seed a different perspective about you in the mind of your ex. With or without a response, that seed will have taken root.

So what do you do to get a response? The answer is you wait. Wait for a few days or even a week or two. You must demonstrate with action that the things you've said in your letter are true. You gave no indication that you needed a response, and every indication that you didn't, so for now your ex may even be testing you. This is a possibility because, and let's face it, our partners often know us better than we know ourselves. If your ex suspects any kind of ploy with your initial contact, they'll be hanging back to see what happens next. So make sure nothing happens next.

You will probably find your ex will contact you within a few days, for this is usually how long it will take for that seed of wonder to grow in their mind before they will just "have to find out." Be wary, however, that they don't use a mutual friend to find the answers that they are seeking. Be on the lookout for strange questions from workmates, family or friends who are also in contact with your ex. Take care not to give anything away to anyone at this point of your life!

If you fail to receive a response from your ex within 7-14 days (you can judge what seems like a fair time frame based on your circumstances and how you feel), then follow up with a very short email that reads:

> Hi Jane,
>
> I sent you a note a week back by snail mail. Just want to know that you got it.
>
> Hope life is treating you good,
>
> Jack

Notice how you aren't saying anything other than asking for a simple acknowledgment. Even if your ex doesn't want to speak with you, the chances are high that he/she won't feel under control or pushed into a corner by replying to such a request. Whatever you do, don't send any email to your ex with a "request read receipt" attached. You absolutely do not want your ex feeling like your spying on them, watching them, or placing pressure on them to reply. Once again, just sit back and wait.

If after another 7-14 days you get no response then remain calm. Remind yourself that perhaps your email could have gone to spam or that your ex is away and not checking email. Or perhaps your ex just didn't know how to respond and is still summoning up the courage. Or perhaps your handwritten note and email has so confused them about what to do that rather than ignoring you they've been going through an intense period of "working out what they want." In other words, never assume the worst! Time is a healer, and patience is its partner! Give your email another 14 days before responding, after which you should write something like this:

Hi Jane,

I hope you're ok. I sent a note by snail mail and also an email and haven't heard from you in over a month. I've been holding off from contacting you again just in case you really don't want to hear from me at all, which is ok if that's what you want, but I'm kind of worried that something else is wrong that I don't know about. I hope you're not sick or hurt or anything. We might not be together anymore and you might still resent me for causing you to leave, but I still think highly of you and want to know you're happy and well, I hope you know that.

I might contact [friends name] or [family member name] just to make sure you're not sick or hurt. Otherwise, please just let me know if you're ok, I'd appreciate it. Even a simple email with "I'm ok, now go away" will do.

Jack

If your ex has been avoiding you, this email is sure to get a response. There's no way they will want you contacting friends or family. If he/she has been ignoring you deliberately you might even receive exactly the kind of email you asked for (a one liner saying "I'm ok, now go away.")

If you do, then that's great because your ex will have responded to you and done exactly what you asked and it gives you a chance to reply, despite the nature of the message. Your reply will open up the opportunity to get the communication lines going again. Bear in mind, however, that if you do get such a response, then you need to be more patient and wait longer than you otherwise might prefer. But it is essential that you do.

Here's how to respond if you do receive such a reply:

LOL! Well at least I know you're ok. ☺

I'll go away now.

Jack

PS. Just make sure you keep in touch from time to time. I know you don't want to hear from me, but I can't just forget you exist even if you want me to. I'll always care you know, even when we're both old, fat, wrinkled, and married to people we haven't met yet. It's up to you, of course, but I do hope you can find it in you to stay friends.

This email is guaranteed to get you a response, but you'll have to send it with the intention of making it your last email.

When you don't get a response

There are some cases where the circumstances of the breakup and the events since have made reconciliation unlikely. There will always be the odd case where no matter how many right moves you make, no matter how good your timing is, your ex will be like a rock hard statue and won't budge from handwritten notes or email contact.

If this is the case, know that your relationship is severely harmed. The chances of getting back with your ex become more remote if he/she still ignores you despite:

- Your handwritten note
- Your follow up emails
- At least 1-2 months have passed
- Enough time has passed for people who know you both to have seen the changes in you and communicated how different you are to your ex

At this point you should definitely question whether it is worth pursuing your ex actively. This doesn't mean you may not get back in the future, but it may mean that you will have to be willing to keep doing what you've been doing to make your own life better and allow your ex even more time between follow up emails. In this instance, send a follow up email after another 2-3 months:

Hi Jane,

It's that guy you used to know :P

Just wondering if you've forgotten that you hate me yet.

Press [reply] on your email to win good karma. :D

Jack

All subsequent emails should include humor.

Should you ever give up on written communication and pick up the phone or engineer a face to face meeting? The answer is no to the phone and yes to the face to face meeting. If your ex is actively ignoring you, a telephone conversation will become awkward. But a face to face meeting, although also awkward, will work in your favor as all preconceptions about you will be broken the moment your ex sees how much you have seemingly changed. You will be unable to convey the degree of this change across the phone and, any attempt to do so will be seen as "mere words".

Face to face contact must appear accidental. Don't suddenly turn up somewhere you never would have gone before just because you know your ex will be there. They call that stalking! Instead, engineer it that you will bump into your ex somewhere comfortable, public, and common. If you know your ex goes to a certain shopping center on a certain night, go there early, purchase something so that you're carrying an item in a bag with a receipt, and then casually bump into him/her and say, "Oh! Sorry, I would have avoided you had I seen you coming…that is what you want, right?"

In all likelihood she'll notice how different you are and say, "No, its ok. How have you been?" - Or something similar.

If she says, "Yes" then you should say, "You know, the fact that you've gone so quiet is a bit sad after all the time we spent together. Surely you can at least tell me off or something? I'll tell you what. I'll buy you a coffee and you can tell me what you think of me. After that, I'll get out of your hair."

If she refuses, say, "Come on, it's a free coffee and a chance to abuse someone, also for free. How bad can five minutes and a free rant be? Do it just once, just this once?" If she pauses say, "Even if I say 'please' and promise to leave you be for all eternity after?"

If you say this with a smile and don't take your eyes off your ex they'll feel compelled to say, "Oh ok." If not, if he/she really is too busy to spend time with you, your request may get her to say, "No, but I'll email you."

Chapter 7: Response Strategies

Whether your ex gets in touch with you immediately after receiving your first handwritten note, after your first email, after your fifth, or after you engineer a public meeting, one way or the other time will ensure that, at some point, you must interact with your ex again. It is this interaction that the make or break of your efforts to win your ex back will unfold. Not only will your ex be closely examining you to see if you are just the same as you always were, but you must say all the right things and take all the right actions to ensure that your ex walks down a new path to wanting to be with you and not just back up the old one.

When to return their contact

If your ex initiates contact with you be sure not to reply immediately. If you receive an email, do not immediately reply. You don't have to wait days or weeks to reply, but you definitely need to pause. The cardinal rule is this:

Before you return any contact, take time out to consider your response.

You must not, under any circumstances, reply in an instant. You should continue to reinforce your lack of desperation. Be courteous by replying in a reasonable time frame, sure, but don't rush it. Remember, rushing anything with your broken relationship could ruin it.

Further, always reply *with the same medium* that you received contact. Don't call your ex if you get an email. Reply by email. Don't email your ex if you get a phone call and a message is left on your answering machine. Return her phone call. Whatever medium your ex contacts you by is the medium your ex wants to converse with you by. So match it.

I see how you feel

Once your ex has initiated contact your first mission is to make sure he/she understands that you acknowledge how they feel. Remember our earlier section on the art of truly listening? Apply it whether or not your ex has contacted you by phone or in writing.

Allow your ex to say whatever it is they want. If it is about your broken relationship, about their own life, or about yours, allow them to say it and do not under any circumstances criticize, condemn or complain about anything they say. Just take it in, acknowledge it, accept they have a valid point of view, tell them so (even if you don't necessarily agree), and then let them pour out more of what they are thinking and feeling.

Be a sponge. Soak up everything they want to say, no matter what it is. Make them feel like you are attentive, caring, and make sure they believe you agree with what they are saying. If all they are doing is talking about their new life, don't start talking about yours. Ask them questions about their life; not personal questions about what they are doing but questions about how they are feeling about what they are doing.

Don't say: "So, have you met anyone else yet?"
Do say: "How are you enjoying being single?"

Don't say: "So, where have you been going on a Thursday night now?"

Do say: "How does it feel to have your Thursday nights back?"

If you keep the conversation surrounding how your ex feels you will give yourself plenty of opportunity to say, "I know how you feel." The more you can say that, without it appearing overtly obvious, the more you can begin to get back "on the same wavelength."

What to do if your ex has met someone else

It is possible that your ex left you for someone else. It is possible that you found out your ex was cheating on you with this person, or it is possible that your ex wasn't cheating but was interested in someone else enough to decide to leave and pursue them. Or, it is possible that your ex has met someone since breaking up with you. And, it is possible that your ex will tell you about this person at some stage, perhaps even during your initial contact.

Your heartfelt desire is to win your ex back and so it will be an emotionally draining experience to hear that someone else has stepped into your shoes and that *your ex has welcomed them.* But here's the thing. You must not, absolutely must not, react poorly.

Earlier in this guide we mentioned that the beginning of any new relationship is the "honeymoon period." Respect that if someone new has entered your ex's life they will be in the most enjoyable phase of any relationship - the beginning. You must accept this because this is the stage where your ex is more likely to defend his or her right to this new relationship because the feelings it is evoking are new, exciting, enjoyable, and distant from the negative feelings they had about your own relationship.

Know that your ex will bring up the subject of a third person with a few things in mind. First, they'll be expecting a negative response from you. They may hope for otherwise, but they'll definitely raise the issue with trepidation and expect you to be sad, angry, to close down, etc. But, they may also raise it because *they want to see if you are jealous.* You won't give your ex what they are looking for. What you want to give your ex is *shock.* The way to do that is to prepare yourself in advance to react exactly how you want to react IF you hear your ex has met someone else. Your reaction should simply be:

"I'm glad you're having fun. He/she better treat you properly!"

As much as this will be hard to deliver, you must deliver it with a genuine tone. If your ex says, "I thought you'd be upset?" you should reply:

"Well I'd prefer it to be me in their shoes, but I just want you to be happy so whatever you want, that's what I want. You know, I messed up in our relationship but I'm not going to repeat that. I won't mess up as your friend! I'm going to be here to support you with everything you do."

Now, this won't stop your ex from seeing this other person, but it will plant a new seed in his/her mind about you. You can rest assured the new person in their life would never be prepared to give your ex this kind of freedom. It will also make the "forbidden fruit" of this other person less attractive. Remember, we want what we can't have - now that your ex realizes he/she can have this new person, the desire for "what they can't have" will diminish, even if they are completely unaware of it. Remember also that your ex left you for more freedom, which you are now offering. All in all, with this kind of an approach you are able to put yourself on a pedestal above anyone your ex could possibly become involved with.

Next, it will also assist to remove many of the negative preconceptions about what went wrong in the relationship. The more your ex thinks about your supportive response, the more your ex will begin to think *you're not like that anymore.* This makes all the qualities they liked about you in the beginning stand out more than those that they didn't like in the end, added to those qualities that they *have now just noticed.* The result is they'll continue seeing this other person, but the whole time they'll be thinking about you, comparing them to you, and wondering more and more about how good you've become.

You may be surprised to learn that in such situations it is far more likely that your ex will get their experience of another person and it is through that experience that they'll realize you are really the person they want.

Let me tell you the story of a friend I know named Derek. Derek was engaged to Rachel for two years before he discovered she was having an affair with her boss. Derek didn't want to lose Rachel but Rachel had already decided she wanted her boss. They had been together for six years, lived together for a year, and even owned a house together, but she left him and moved in with her boss. Derek fought to get her to stay and was devastated when she left. He thought his life was all over and became very depressed. He didn't know what to do and, at one point, contemplated suicide.

Instead, I gave him the very advice I've outlined in this book. So he sent his ex a handwritten note just as we've explained. She telephoned him immediately upon receiving it and thanked him. At the time, she told him that she was happy living with her boss and that she was pleased he was now good with it. He repeated what we've just said here, explaining to her that he knew he'd messed up but that he wanted to be her friend and promised to be the best friend she could ask for. She told him *she wanted to stay friends too.*

Nothing happened for two weeks. During that time, Derek began to also follow these guidelines herein. In only two weeks he began bodybuilding and found himself a new job. He got a haircut, threw out his old clothes and purchased new clothes. He met some new friends at the gym and at his new workplace and began to feel good about himself again. He even went on two comparison dates.

Two weeks later Rachel called out of the blue. She asked Derek how he was and Derek replied, "I'm great! Life is actually getting really good for me. How are you?" Rachel replied, "I don't know. Things just aren't the same." The conversation led to an agreement by both to meet up for a coffee the next day.

When they met, Rachel admitted to Derek that she'd been thinking a lot about him and about what she'd left. She told him that her boss was nice enough but that living with him wasn't the same as *"living with you."* Rachel then started crying and she began to admit all the mistakes *she'd made* even though when she left she had told Derek it was all because of mistakes he had made.

But here's the cruncher. Because Derek had taken it upon himself to start making changes, by the time this meeting occurred, he was feeling good about his life. He was no longer feeling as desperate and as upset that Rachel was gone. In fact, he had met a girl at the gym that he liked. He hadn't said anything to her yet, but he was planning to. In other words, Derek was no longer desperate to have Rachel back.

What do you think happened? Rachel was pouring her heart out and hinting that she wanted to come back, but Derek was just listening. He listened and said, "I'm sorry it's not going well for you." But because he wasn't desperate he didn't say, "Come back to me." He wasn't sure if he wanted Rachel back and so he never suggested or hinted at it. The result, Rachel had to do it. She blurted it out in no uncertain terms: "Derek, would you take me back?"

Can you see how Derek barely had to do a thing to completely shift Rachel's mind from blaming him and wanting to be with someone else to the complete opposite perspective! All he did was exercise the guidance laid out in this guide and a little patience.

Interestingly, Derek did not take Rachel back. In fact, he had been so hurt by Rachel leaving that he took great pleasure in saying, "I'm not ready for that yet, but I'll be here for you if you need me." One week later Derek started dating the girl from the gym. Three weeks later he heard from Rachel again who told him she had moved out of her boss's house into a flat with another girl friend and quit her job. Another week after that and Rachel started dating another guy. Derek and Rachel both dated different people for almost six months before they both became single again and got back together - and now they are happily married.

Of course, I'm not suggesting you follow the exact same path. The story of Derek and Rachel is used merely to illustrate that even when you think all is lost because someone else has moved onto the scene, if you play your cards right, it can be the very thing that solidifies your relationship with your ex in the future. The key, of course, is to prepare for such news in advance. You don't want to be shocked with the news; you want to shock with your response to the news. It's that simple.

Now, it is also possible that the person your ex has met may turn out to be someone your ex wants to stay with. If that is the case, there is nothing you can do differently except what has been laid out so far. You can't do anything about it in the beginning because that is the honeymoon period. And you can't do anything about it later because if two people click, a third person makes no difference. All you can do is follow the guidelines laid out and live your life while being patient. Fortunately, however, the chances are in your favor that your approach will leave your ex thinking about you often and in a positive frame of light. That in itself works against her new relationship and her partner will pick up on it. Also, as soon as their new partner slips up (and inevitably we all do), your ex will come running back to you.

When to suggest a get together?

One of the biggest mistakes made by those seeking to win their partner back is to allow their hopes to sky rocket the moment their ex returns contact. This is a big mistake as it inevitably leads to asking your ex to meet up the moment you get even the slightest hint that they might be interested in doing so - and often when you are desperate you may see such a hint where there is none. Here's the rule:

Don't be the initiator.

By that, I mean don't ask your ex to meet up. Don't say, "Want to grab a coffee?" Don't say, "We should get together and talk." Don't do or say anything to initiate a meeting because the moment you do your ex will have to think: do I want to do this?

Instead, you want your ex to think, "Does he/she want to meet me?" This is the thought that desires a "yes" and so you must be patient and allow your ex to initiate any meeting. Remember, your ex left you and so it is your ex that must initiate the comeback. Don't try to push in early because you think things are going well. The longer you wait the more your ex will begin to wonder if you're ever going to ask. If your ex is leaning back in your direction, he/she will begin to get concerned when you fail to ask to meet up and, by nature, they'll do it for you - just as Rachel did for Derek.

If your ex prompts then by all means ask. For example, if your ex says, "I see that new café has opened on Smith St." then you can reply, "Really? I haven't been there yet. If you want to try their coffee sometime let me know." If your ex was looking to meet up, they'll reply, "Well, do you want to meet up there for a coffee?" If they weren't, then you won't get rejected because you haven't directly asked for a meeting. Either way you will win because one way or another the seed will have been planted that you're willing to meet up *if your ex asks.*

On that latter note, always be aware that just because your ex abandoned you that they aren't wondering if you would take them back. In the story of Derek and Rachel, it was Rachel who left and it was Rachel who was put in a position of wondering if Derek would take her back. Your job is to add that mystery to your friendship. As long as your ex isn't sure if you would take them back or not you'll be more of a "forbidden fruit" than not. Remember, what people don't think they can have they are more likely to want.

Once things are going well and your ex initiates a meeting and you agree to meet up, there are a few things you must do and a few things to avoid.

Three's a crowd and familiarity is old

Make sure you avoid meeting your ex around their family or their friends. Definitely do not allow your first meeting to take place anywhere that you will both be interrupted, either by the environment or by other people. For example, don't go to the movies, don't go to a sporting event, don't visit your ex at her family home, don't meet your ex while he/she is at a bar with their best friend, and so forth. If you meet up you must do so in a private setting where you both can completely concentrate on each other. It can be a public café or even a restaurant, or a park bench - so long as you both will have no risk of interruption. The key is to make sure your ex can concentrate fully on you without distraction or without worrying about what those around him/her think.

Next, make sure that the meeting duration is fixed in advance. Advise your ex you'll only have an hour because of some other commitment. Be sure that this is explained in advance. This is why a coffee is the ideal way to meet up because café's are typically places that you only stay as long as you're drinking your coffee!

Next, make sure you don't go somewhere you used to go together either when you were together or when you started dating for the first time. You absolutely must avoid any place that has a previous association to you. The reason for this is that you can't be sure whether or not your ex has a positive or negative association to you with certain places, smells, or surroundings. Instead, you want to impress the "new you" and to do that you need a "new place" to impress a "new association".

The new location you choose should be somewhere that isn't overtly romantic, that is relatively quiet, and that allows for a certain amount of activity, either visually or physically. For example, a café has people coming and going and plenty of social chatter going on around you. Or, you might sit by the river and watch boats and birds go by while you chat. Or, you might go for a walk around a park, etc.

The trick with your meeting place is that it must be new. You can allow your ex to choose the place, but be careful if you do. Make sure you find a good excuse to meet somewhere else if your ex suggests a place that will detract from your concentration on each other or potentially involve her family and friends. For example, if your ex says, "I'm going to the ice skating rink on Saturday, you should come" is a definite no-no because you'll know it is something pre-organized and therefore she won't be alone and able to concentrate on you. If she says, "Want to meet up at [the café you always used to go to]" you should say, "Actually I've found an awesome little café that's even better that I think you'll love, let's meet there instead!"

Raising issues

When you meet with your ex for the first time after a breakup it is almost inevitable that things will be said that will be emotionally charged. The first step to avoiding this is to refuse to raise any issues yourself. Make sure that your priority is to listen and respond to what your ex is talking about. Don't actively raise any previous relationship issues yourself. Be sure to remember what's past has past. You are only interested in moving forward.

Of course, you may find yourself drawn into a conversation about past issues because your ex is raising them. After all, you can't just ignore or skirt around issues that your ex is highlighting as important, and nor can you brush off anything your ex raises *because he/she will feel unimportant if you do.* Just remember the advice given earlier: you must put yourself in your ex's shoes and acknowledge his/her feelings, accept any responsibility that they directly or indirectly fling at you, and say, "I understand how you feel." Don't allow yourself to be drawn into an argument. If you feel yourself getting emotionally charged, breathe, count to 10, and then say, "I understand."

If your ex gets overbearingly emotional or intense with the way in which they approach raising your relationship issues you should already be prepared for it. Don't react how you have always reacted. Demonstrate you've changed by showing that you're only interested in helping and improving your relationship and not defending yourself. You do want your ex back right? Then show that you've changed by being different and by seeing everything as they see it. Listen, pause, and always respond with empathy.

If your ex says, "You ruined our relationship."
Respond, "One thing is for sure, I'm not going to ruin our friendship."

If your ex says, "If you hadn't done that, I'd still be with you."
Respond, "I'll have to live with that mistake forever."

If your ex says, "I loved you so much, now I just hate you for everything."
Respond, "Not as much as I hate myself for screwing everything up."

If your ex says, "You were such a bastard to me, all the time."
Respond, "I was stupid and lost sight of what mattered. I made you feel bad and I'm sorry for that. I won't forget that by being a stupid bastard I lost you. I'm not going to make the mistake of being a bastard to anyone ever again. "

Get the drift?

"We were great, but not that great"

Have you noticed that much of what has been discussed so far is about using reverse psychology to say one thing that leads to another? We'll discuss more psychological weapons that you can use in the next section but before we do here is one you can use right from the very first contact you have (not in your handwritten note, but once your ex initiates contact).

Most break-ups don't go that well. There is usually yelling, arguing, crying, and a whole host of emotions that both partners will direct at each other. Considering that you are reading this guide, it is likely that you begged your partner not to leave, asked them to stay, and pleaded with them to give you a second chance. However it went down, the odds are your partner is pretty sure that, because they left you, *you lost the best thing you've ever had or ever will have.*

You may even feel exactly the same way right at this moment. You may feel that your partner was "the one" and that by losing them you've lost your one and only chance at a happy life with your perfect partner. Your ex doesn't think this way because your ex left. Your ex may realize that you were great, but in the end all the negatives about you outweighed the positives and *that's why they left.* So as it stands, the only thought your ex can have about what you've lost is that they left you and therefore *you lost.*

Upon initiating contact you can be reasonably sure that this perspective will not have changed. It is unlikely, even if your ex wants to come back to you, that they won't *you lost them.* This is also true if your ex isn't sure if you would take them back. It is virtually an unavoidable situation of perspective that when one partner leaves that they don't think the other is the person who lost, and not them.

Once again, you must plant an all new seed of "mystery" by shocking your ex into believing their perspective is an illusion. You can do this very simply.

You can do it in writing, or you can do it in person. It doesn't matter when you do it so long as it is after your ex contacts you of their own volition. When they do, you can say something like this at any point:

"Even though we had some issues I thought we used to have a great relationship, but you're right, some parts of it weren't that great. If they were, you wouldn't have left. I never thought I'd say this but I see now why we had to break up. If we didn't, I may never have stopped making those mistakes. At least now I know what not to do with my relationships in the future and I'll never hurt anyone again like I hurt you, never!"

Notice what such a statement achieves:

- It conveys your ex made the right decision
- It conveys responsibility for what happened
- It conveys that you think your relationship could have been better
- It conveys you don't intend making the same mistakes
- It conveys that you've changed for the better
- It conveys that you didn't see before what you see now
- It conveys that you are not what your ex left anymore

Most of all, it conveys that you now view your past relationship as something that was great but something that could have been better, and that your next relationship will be better than the one you had with your ex. The reverse psychology of this is that it plants a seed in the mind of your ex that everything they left you for was right, but that it now no longer applies. The result is your ex will, on a conscious or subconscious level, feel like it is *they who have lost* the chance to have a future great relationship with you that, in the beginning, was exactly what they wanted.

You'll find such a statement will elicit a response from your ex that will give you a subtle indication that your reverse psychology has started to work. Any statement from your ex like either of the following is a step in the right direction:

"If only you'd said that when we were together!"
"I'm glad to hear you say that, even if it's too late."
"Great, you had to hurt me to have a good relationship with someone else."
"Well, I never thought I'd hear those words."
"I only hope you mean that."
"You've really changed, you know that?"

"That's a far cry from the way you were when we broke up."
"Wow, there's hope for you yet."
Etc.

The all knowing thirty party

Many people suffering breakups underestimate the frequency through which one partner may keep tabs on the other using mutual acquaintances. If you think that your ex will never come into contact with any friends of yours or work colleagues whom she has met in the past, think again. Make sure that you constantly stay vigilant for the possibility that somehow, somewhere, your ex will talk to someone you know; a friend, a family member, a work colleague - anyone.

Make sure that you *never say anything to anyone that you wouldn't want your ex to hear.*

Don't say to your friends, "Hey, I'm reading this guide on how to get my ex back and there are some really cool weapons of reverse psychology I'm going to use." What do you think will happen if one of these friends bumps into your ex? They may say, "Look, I shouldn't say this, but be careful. [Your name] is reading a book about how to trick you into getting back together."

If you allow this situation to occur you'll lose your ex forever.

Don't say to your ex's best friend, "I can't live without him/her, can you make sure you say something to make him/her come back to me?!" Your ex's best friend has your ex's best interests in mind over yours! They might go straight to your ex and say, "He/she's so pathetic, you're better off without the sniveling fool."

It doesn't matter who they are, people always want to have their say. Everyone your ex comes into contact with will have something to say about you and the breakup. Make sure any ammunition you give them is exactly what you'd want them to feed to your ex. Better yet, make sure you only give mystery by responding only with questions. If they feed more mystery to your ex, your ex will wonder about you even more. For example, imagine you bump into your ex's mother in the street. Instead of saying, "I miss her so much" you should say, "How are you? How is [her husband, your ex's dad]? I miss seeing you guys." Don't even ask about your ex! You can also say, "Things are pretty good. I'm getting fitter now because I joined the gym and have met a few new friends to keep me busy now that I'm on my own."

What do you think her mother will do/think? She'll go back to your ex and tell her that you're doing pretty well for yourself. Since you highlighted the fact that you *miss her and the family* more than you mentioned anything specifically about your ex she'll be more inclined to respect you and translate that respect in the way she speaks about you to your ex. Clearly, that will also shift your ex's perspective dramatically.

You should apply the same principle to anyone you meet who might, in the future, come into contact with your ex. Make sure that anything they might say is about how good you are and what you're doing rather than asking about your ex. In fact, don't ask about your ex at all. Don't say, "What's he/she up to?" Just don't say anything. Then when your ex asks their friend or family member, "Did he/she ask about me?" they'll feel rejected to find out you didn't and they'll wonder why. They'll instantly jump to the conclusion you've met someone else and that in turn will inspire them to want to contact you to find out. Or, they'll ask their friend/family member to ask you if they see you again. One way or the other, you'll find someone in the future asking you to hand over more details about what you're up to - but don't give them. Answer with a mystery; answer with another question.

If asked, "So, I heard you're out on the town with someone new?"
Say, "Really? What *exactly* did you hear?"

If asked, "I heard you've made new friends. Anyone I should know about?"
Say, "Not really. Just some people I met through the gym."

If asked, "Do you miss [your ex]?"
Say, "Probably as much as he/she misses me."

Chapter 8: Psychological Weapons

The Power of Saying "I Won't Let Myself Miss You"

We've just discussed how to handle a third party asking whether or not you miss your ex. This question, or something very similar, is quite a common way for your ex to find out not only how their leaving has impacted you, but what you're doing now that they are gone without having to contact you of their own volition.

By answering with a statement that says, "I feel the same as they do" you prevent your ex from learning anything at all - but you do establish a kind of rapport. If your ex really misses you, he/she will think that you really miss them too. If they aren't missing you, then they'll be dismayed to learn that you probably don't miss them either. Either way, if they harbored a belief that you had any kind of different feeling than what they did, their illusion will be shattered. Or they won't believe you, in which case they'll be compelled to find out the truth *by speaking with you themselves.* Remember, each time you break a pre-conception in your ex's mind you plant the seed of mystery and wonder.

There is, however, another way to go about this. Rather than responding with a statement that neither confirms nor denies whether or not you are missing your ex, you can play the reverse psychology game of saying one thing while meaning another. Here's what to say if you are asked by a friend, family member or even directly by your ex if you miss him or her:

"Actually, to be honest, [your ex's name] walked out on me. [Your ex's name] doesn't want to be a part of my life. So I've been doing everything I can to make sure that I don't miss them. You know, because I have to."

Such a statement, whether delivered directly or from a third party, will not directly infer that you don't miss your ex, but it will infer that you are actively taking action to get over your ex. It also adds mystery by inferring that you are taking action, whatever that may be, to make sure that you get over your ex leaving. Again, this will make them wonder what exactly you are doing - and who you are doing it with - to avoid missing them. It also removes any pre-conception that you may be desperate to get your ex back as it demonstrates you've fully accepted your ex has gone and you're not going to let their departure ruin your life.

At first your ex might be dismayed to hear that you won't allow yourself to miss them, but the more they brood on hearing this news the more they'll begin to realize that the reason you're not missing them is that you are keeping yourself too busy to think about them. As they do, they'll be compelled to throw a spanner in the works and the easy way to do that is to contact you. They'll reason, either consciously or subconsciously, that if they contact you *you'll have no choice but to think about them.* In many cases when a partner leaves they want you to suffer, and making sure that you can't stop thinking about them can become a driving motive. While not one of good intention, if you engineer your partner to do this, the fact that they are contacting you and thinking about how you feel is at least a step towards giving you further opportunity to demonstrate the "new you."

Remember, people always want what they can't have. The less your ex thinks you're thinking about them, the more they'll want you back. The less they think you miss them, the more they'll want you to miss them; the more they think about you the more they'll miss you too. The more your ex has to think about what you're doing, who you're doing it with, and whether or not you still care or wonder about him/her, the more power you gain.

Misery is the deal breaker; happiness the deal maker

We've already fully discussed why it is important that you concentrate on changing and improving yourself personally and your life in totality. Every single quality that fits on the positive and constructive side of the scale is attractive, while everything else is unattractive and repelling. The only way you'll win your ex back is to think, say and do everything you can that makes you and everyone else around you feel good.

Obviously you don't want your ex to think you are happy because he/she is gone, so there is a fine line you must tread here. On one hand you want your ex to perceive that you've changed for the better and to do that you'll need to show how much you can enjoy life now, while on the other you want to indirectly hint that there's room for your ex to move back into your life just enough that your ex will eventually ask you to meet up or ask you if they can come back.

Fortunately, this is a fine line that is quite easy to tread. It is as simple as this: don't be miserable.

You don't have to be the local clown, the world's top comedian, a ray of sunshine, or laugh and joke about everything that comes your way. You don't need to grin from ear to ear or make light of everything you see, do or hear. You don't have to be the most positive person on the block. You just have to ensure that in all your interactions you make sure that the way you behave doesn't bring anyone down. The key is to avoid being depressed, avoid criticizing, avoid complaining, and avoid appearing miserable.

If you appear miserable or depressed *it is a deal breaker.* No one wants to be around someone who brings them down and this is especially so when it comes to spending your life with a soul-mate. Instead, you have to bring people up. If you avoid being depressed and miserable, at least by appearance, you avoid bringing people down. When you interact from a foundation of misery you end up saying all the wrong things and giving all the wrong body language. When someone is down in the dumps people offer support, but when someone stays down in the dumps and never changes, people no longer support - they are repelled. The opposite is true.

Earlier it was suggested that one way to distract you from wallowing in misery is to embark on a quest of self improvement and personal change. It is through such a process that you can bring yourself up in both mood and outlook, and it is through this that you can bring others up too. If you skipped over that section lightly, go back and re-read it. It is very important that you take every step you can to shift your perception from one of "I've lost my world and I can't live without my ex" to "now I have a whole new world at my fingertips and can do anything I choose!" Remember, a compelling life will compel your ex back. A life filled with void because your ex is no longer there won't compel him or her to return.

Now, let me just say I completely get it if you think that you can't be a positive, humorous or happy person. After all, your world just crumbled and right now you're probably feeling as bad as you ever have, if not worse. In fact you can probably rattle off a thousand reasons why you just can't be happy anymore and, for that matter, don't want to be.

But here's the thing.

Happiness is fleeting. It's not a permanent thing. The only time laughter is permanent is when you're insane and locked in an asylum! The trick is not to be Jovial Jim every second of every waking moment. What we're talking about is how you interact with others. When you're alone you can distract yourself as much as you like, but there'll still be times where you can't help but sit down and feel bad. There'll be times where you lose all motivation to do anything, where you'll cry; perhaps times when you'll break something in anger or frustration. That's fine. Just don't let those times consume your daily life.

Your goal is to allow the miserable, depressed and unhappy times to have their moment *when you're alone.* If you do, and you let them come and go and pass quickly, then they'll do you no harm. If you allow such emotions to be expressed around others, well, that's when they become damaging. Don't let negative emotions or states of mind have a negative impact on your life. You can't avoid them; you know that, so express them when they can do the least damage.

Most of all, NEVER express them when around or in contact with your ex. Your ex must think that you've changed for the better. Your ex must perceive a warmer, more constructive, more positive thinking individual who is trying to embrace the enjoyable, humorous side of life. Don't give any indication that you have any reason to hate life. Don't admit to being depressed in private. Don't show any weakness at all. Be a compelling individual. If you have to pretend, then pretend like the best actor in the world pretends, and then let your guard down when you are alone.

Of course your aim is to be happy as much as you can, but right about now that's easier said than done. So make an effort to pretend for now and let your true happiness begin to grow in time - it certainly will when your ex sees the difference and returns to you!

The longer the distance, the greater the pull

Just as human beings always want what they can't have, so to do they never miss anyone as much as when they're not around. This is another reason why when you want your ex to truly desire to come back to you it is imperative that you allow a distance to grow between you both.

In a sense your mission is to turn the tables. Your ex left you, and so it is up to you to send a loud and clear message that you've accepted the situation so well that now you are actually the one doing the leaving. You're leaving behind the bad times, you're leaving behind the desperation to get back together, you're leaving behind the need to have your ex in your life, and you're leaving behind everything about your old life - which includes the old you - that you don't want anymore.

Again, it must be reiterated, patience is your best friend. You must exercise patience at all cost. Realize that the longer you go without contacting your ex the greater the chance of winning your ex back. The less your ex is aware of what you're doing, the more they'll want to know. It really is that simple.

Many people make the mistake of arguing this point. They allow their fear of being lonely or fear of losing their ex forever to formulate an argument against patience. They ignore the old adage that "time is the great healer" and they convince themselves that if they don't force contact as soon as they can then they'll lose their ex forever. Sure, in the very rare instance they may succeed, but in 99% of cases they do not. By forcing their way into the life of the very person who made the decision that they didn't want them there, they reinforce that decision tenfold. Don't reinforce your ex's decision by clinging and acting in desperation.

Let the distance between you both grow. View distance as being similar to an elastic band. The band will stretch but eventually it will reach a point where it will either snap or, if you let go at just the right time, it will rebound. The techniques discussed so far are all about having patience so that you can initiate contact with your ex, or get your ex to contact you, with perfect timing. Any rushed contact *is not perfect timing.* Allow the distance to sever thoughts about how bad your relationship was and replace them with thoughts of "what's he/she doing these days?" and "wow, he/she's really changed!" It only takes a few weeks but, even if you have to wait months, that's ok too. Your goal is to win your ex back and keep them forever, not just win them back today and lose them again tomorrow.

The projection method

Another method of "win your ex back psychological warfare" is the act of projecting onto your ex all the positive qualities that you know they desire to personally have. What are these qualities? They are the opposite of everything your ex has ever complained about. Remember the list you created at the beginning of the book of all the things that you should have done in your relationship? These hold the key to all the positive thoughts, words and actions your ex really wants to see you do and hear you say.

If your ex complained that you never gave him/her attention, then every chance you have give it to them, starting by hanging on every word that they utter. Then ask questions about everything they say and reinforce that you're listening and care about the thing that they are talking about. After all, they do - that's why they're talking about it!

If you struggle with how to project onto your ex the qualities he/she wants, then think about the whole scenario as a subtle way of laying on the compliments.

For example:

Your ex says, "I really hated the way you were treating me."
You reply, "I understand and apologize. To be honest, I think you are one of the best people I've ever known and I wish I'd always treated you the way you deserved to be treated."

Or your ex says: "I think breaking up was the best thing we could have done. Now I'm finally getting time to study again."
You reply: "You always said you wanted to study again and you're damn good at it, so that's great."

Or your ex says, "You know, it's for the best that we broke up."
You say: "Well, I can see why you left and though I wish there had been another way, you were completely right. I should have listened to you more often to be honest. But I'm listening now. If you say it's for the best then I agree."

If your ex says: "These days I'm getting more into volleyball."
You say: "That doesn't surprise me; you'd be great at that."

If your ex says: "I'm going to start studying computer programming."
You say: "Well you're one of the smartest people I know so I think you'll love doing that."

The projection method is not only about reinforcing what your ex thinks but also emphasizing your ex's greatest qualities. However, you have to be sure that you don't make it obvious that all you're trying to do is impress by compliment. Only ever project a complimentary comment in response to a comment raised by your ex. If you ex says "Y", you emphasize how right he/she is about "Y" and tie it into another attribute about your ex that you know will make them feel good about themselves.

The key here is to make your ex feel important, but don't go overboard. It is the rare or obscure projections that make all the difference. The moment it appears like you're handing out compliments with an ulterior motive every compliment you've issued will become worthless.

When it comes to reinforcing how special your ex is by emphasizing their best qualities, you should remind yourself that the reason you're doing it is to make your ex feel good about speaking with you once again. The moment your ex left you it was because they had decided being around you wasn't that good for them. But if every time they speak with you they come away feeling great, the view they had that prompted them to leave will slowly get replaced by a view that prompts them to return.

After all, we all want to be around people that make us feel good and your ex is no different.

Something has changed

We've already talked about how creating mystery and wonder about the "new you" and your "new life" can compel your ex to contact you to find out the details. Earlier we also touched upon doing this by providing a subtle hint that something about your life has changed for the better *and that is why you're actually quite happy right now*, again to compel the interest of your ex further. For this key tactic to work you must *actually have something in your life* that has changed it for the better.

Find something that compels you: a new hobby, a new toy, a new interest or two, and immerse yourself in it. Then, when your ex tries to find out what this thing - or this person - is, then you can legitimately smile and talk about it with passion. If you fail to talk about the "mystery something" with conviction when your ex comes asking, you'll fail to compel your ex to believe that your life is getting interesting.

Remember, you have to be compelled by your own life before your ex or anybody else will be.

Chapter 9: The Second Chance

"I'm not ready yet"

We've already stressed the importance of having patience and allowing time for the issues of the past to begin to fade. We've also emphasized that patience is required for the new, compelling side of who you are and what your life is becoming to slowly take root in the mind of your ex. You also know that if you rush a reunion the chances are you'll blow your chance to ignite a new spark and start an all new and fresh relationship with your ex that will last. So what happens if your ex comes knocking on your door within days of leaving you? Do you take him/her back without a second thought?

The answer to this question will depend heavily on your individual circumstances, but you should proceed with the utmost of caution if you find yourself in this position. The reason why you must be cautious is that the thoughts and feelings that prompted your ex to leave in the first place will still be prevalent in his/her mind. Not enough time will have passed for them to have faded and not enough time will have passed for your ex to have started thinking radically different about who you are. Additionally, not enough time will have passed for you to have made major changes in your life. If your ex recently left you, then you should consider allowing the break to continue, at least for a short period, otherwise you run the very real risk of getting back together and breaking up again in the near future.

Remember the story of Derek and Rachel? Derek wanted Rachel back so badly, but when Rachel asked if he would take her back, he declined. He was able to decline because he had made himself interested in his own life to the point that he no longer feared losing Rachel. Sure, he still wanted her back, but he knew if he simply gave in and said "yes" the moment she asked, then at some point in the future she could leave him again and possibly for good. Derek knew that if he said "yes" then many of the issues that he and Rachel originally broke up over would not be resolved because he had not allowed enough time for her to get over him, and for him to get over her. Furthermore, Rachel was still living with her boss when she asked if she could return. Derek knew that this meant, in a sense, that he would be the rebound and as we discussed earlier, rebound relationships rarely last. Instead, Derek said he wasn't ready. Rachel, having openly admitted she no longer wanted to be with her boss then prompted herself to move in with a friend. But Derek and Rachel kept contact and, in time, married. So always know that if you and your ex are meant to be, then a little more time apart may be what strengthens your future together rather than breaks it.

If you find yourself too scared and fearful of losing your ex forever by saying you're not ready yet, then know that *it is you who isn't ready yet.* You must fully accept life without your ex in order to win a life with your ex that will last forever. You can say something like this:

"I really want to, I do. But you really hurt me when you left. I know I caused it all and deserved it but that didn't stop my heart from breaking when you left. It's repairing though. Besides, if we get back together I want us to be the greatest of friends before we become anything more. Can we do that? Can we just grow our friendship for now?"

Your ex will be disappointed but two things will have happened. The first is that you will have taken a position of power in the relationship because no longer has your ex left you, but you've left him/her. Now you are the person who is "hard to get". You are the person who is calling the shots. But best of all, you know your ex wants you back. That means if you play your cards right, you can grow that friendship and get back together faster than you seem to be letting on. But, for now, it will work in your favor to say, "I'm not ready yet." She'll be disappointed but she'll be compelled to say "yes" to your request to become "the greatest friends first."

Of course, taking this approach also depends on your decision that you will offer a second chance, so let's talk about that now.

Deciding there will be a second chance

The moment your ex left you something became very clear: your ex made a decision that their life was better off without you in it. The moment your ex makes a decision to return, you must make something very clear to yourself: that your ex's life will be better off with you back in it. If your ex asks you directly, you can phrase this question to him/her:

"Do you think you'll be better off if we're back together?"

You know the answer will be "yes" because your ex has already made the decision. But by getting your ex to openly state the fact is a psychological way of gaining more power over the relationship. Remember, your ex took 100% of the power in your relationship when they ended it. So, to counter-balance this, you must take 100% of the power that restarts it. The moment your ex admits that they'll be better off with you, everything from that point becomes your decision and yours alone.

Even though by this point you may have waited months for your ex to come back to you, perhaps even as long as a year or two, you should pause and consider whether or not *you'll be better off.* This is where you must face some honest truths. Until now you've been taking the approach of accepting complete responsibility for what happened. You've taken all the blame your ex threw at you on the chin and completely shifted any previous stance you had to one that aligns perfectly with the viewpoint of your ex. But remember, you did this to win your ex back. The moment you ex says he/she wants to come back, and the moment they admit they are going to be better off with you in their life, *you've got your ex back if you want them back.* At this point, you need to make sure that you don't just take them back and for the rest of your life your ex gets to walk all over you, blaming you for this and that and expecting you to take full responsibility for everything that might go wrong now or in the future.

And you won't have to. Since the power in your relationship has now been handed completely to you, and since you know your ex wants back because they feel they'll be better off, use that power to lay some ground rules. This is your chance to openly discuss those things that *you feel need to change* too. As soon as you're ready to give that second chance, you should say:

"I really want to get back with you too, but before we do, there are just a couple of things we need to make sure we get right. Is that ok?"

Then ask for your ex's agreement on those things that bothered you that remain unresolved in your own mind and that you feel may continue to remain unresolved unless addressed. If there were past issues that you think have now dissolved, don't raise them. There is no point stirring up the hornet's nest for issues that may no longer have any place in your life. However, for issues that you feel may still crop up, especially those that you feel your ex contributed to for which you have until now taken complete blame, you should raise them carefully. For example, imagine that one reason your ex left was that they felt you didn't communicate properly while the truth is you felt that they were the one that didn't communicate. This is what you can say:

"You know how you think I didn't talk to you openly enough before? Well, I want to make sure that doesn't happen again. So if you think I'm not being open at any point, can you please tell me immediately? I need you to be open with me if I am to be open with you, can you do that?"

And:

"You know how you hated it when I used to go silent? Sometimes not saying anything is the best way I can deal with things and it gives me a chance to get my thoughts straight. If that happens again, can you promise to ask me if I'm just trying to collect my thoughts rather than ignoring you? Because I'll never ignore you, ever, and I want you to know that. Is that ok?"

And:

"If we get back together, can you promise me that if you ever have an issue you'll raise it straight away?"

Whatever issue you have, try to raise it in a way that makes it a *shared* issue. But be sure to raise it before you agree to give your ex a second chance.

Once you agree to let your ex back into your life, then it's time for a first date and you should phrase it like that to your ex:

"Well, before we get back together again, I think we should do this properly. Would you like to go on a 'first date' with me?"

A first date, again

If you've already met up with your ex numerous times prior to deciding to get back together, you must remember that the very next meeting is your first date. If you want the spark to really ignite in your new relationship you will need to allow the relationship to flow just as if it were a brand new one. That includes making your next date a real first date.

This is where many people make monumental mistakes. They do exactly what they did before. They fall back into old habits. They go to familiar places. They think: "I got my ex back!" and then proceed to act as if nothing had ever changed in the first place. They push the "reset button" and expect that the gap between then and now was just a break to be forgotten about. Don't make the same mistake.

Make your first date special. Treat your ex as if he/she is a brand new person in your life that you're trying to woo. You want to do something new, something special, something that places a great deal of attention on your ex and that is designed to be fun and exciting. Above all else, make it all a complete mystery to your ex, minute by minute. Never let on exactly what is coming next.

If you are going to the museum, don't tell your ex until you are in the museum. If you are going to a restaurant, it's a secret until you are in the restaurant. And so on.

Treat your first date as a chance to get to know your ex. If you think that sounds stupid because you already know your ex, think again. If you really knew your ex you wouldn't have broken up! This is your chance to ask your ex as many questions about him/her as you can think of. Find out what they've been up to while you've been gone, what new interests they've taken up or thought about, and what they want out of their life. Even if you think you know the answer, ask anyway.

If your ex says, "You already know that!"
Reply with a smile, "Well, I'm not going to take anything about you for granted ever again, so you're going to have answer by telling me something I don't know!"

By treating your first date as a fresh new start you should also find it a lot easier to avoid talking about anything from the past. On your first date your past no longer exists. It is, after all, a first date. If the past does get brought up, either by you accidentally or deliberately by your ex, make sure you find a way to laugh at it.

If your ex says, "Why couldn't you have been like this before?"
Say with a smile, "Because I needed you to dump that guy first, he sucked."

Laugh off any references to the past, and then immediately shift your attention back to the present.

You're back together

If you've followed the guidelines in this book then your life will have undergone major transformation since the time your ex left you. From what was first a major catastrophe, your ex's departure will have inspired a great many positive and constructive changes to who you are as a person and how you conduct yourself in life in general.

When combined with the contact, response, and psychological techniques provided herein, your personal transformation will have enabled you to not only attract your ex back into your life, but to secure a first date and re-establish a brand new warm, loving, sharing and healthy relationship that is superior to any that you had before. Not only that, but you'll now be fully equipped to make sure your new relationship prospers over the long term.

It is also possible that through your transformation a whole host of additional possibilities opened before you, possibilities that did not include reigniting the spark with your ex. If that is the case then "You Can Win Your Ex Back" will still have achieved its end goal of helping you get *exactly what you want in a relationship.* If that meant letting your ex go and igniting an all new spark with an all new partner - or staying single to pursue your new dream life - then you should be very pleased about that.

Of course, it is also very probable that you'll read this last section of the book before any major transformations have taken place. You may still be searching for new hobbies, new interests and a new course in life. You may yet to have sent your first handwritten note. You may yet to have received a reply from you ex and may still be awaiting the chance to use reverse psychology on your ex's family or friends. If that is the case then it is highly recommended that you start over. Read the book from the beginning and make sure that no stone gets left unturned.

Commit yourself to embarking on a process of self discovery. Make sure you understand the subtle psychological nuances that you must employ in order to support rather than sabotage a new relationship with your ex. Make sure that you do find a passion for a new hobby, interest, or sport. Get yourself into a position where all the changes you are making to your life are interesting and compelling and where each day you wake up thinking, "I'm going to do *this* today and maybe *that* too!"

Get yourself to a position where you are doing so many new activities and making so many changes to your life that you are simply way too distracted to lament your past. If you finish one self-improvement book this week start another next week. Visit your friends *but don't talk about your ex.* Talk about what your friends have been up to and the new things in your life that you're up to. Be a compelling, interesting and above all else life adding rather than life draining individual to be around.

Do all of these things, following the steps outlined in this guide, and you are guaranteed to become a more compelling, attractive individual. Through this your ex will come to realize that the reasons they decided to leave you no longer apply, and that all the good aspects about who you are and what you do are still there, only now there are even more of them.

Exercise patience. Allow time to heal old wounds. Avoid anything that is destructive to your health or your life. Embrace everything that is not. Be the person your ex wants you to be and merge that with the person you know you can be.

So start now and let the rest unfold in its due course. If you suspend your old beliefs and habits and replace them with what you have learned in this guide, a future with a great relationship supporting you is a given.

It all begins with you.

You can win your ex back.

Printed in Great Britain
by Amazon.co.uk, Ltd.,
Marston Gate.